SUMMER OVER AUTUMN

SUMMER
OVER AUTUMN

A Small Book of Small-Town Life

Howard Mansfield

BAUHAN PUBLISHING
PETERBOROUGH, NEW HAMPSHIRE
2017

Library of Congress Cataloging-in-Publication Data

Names: Mansfield, Howard, author.
Title: A small book of small-town life / Howard Mansfield.
Description: Peterborough, New Hampshire : Bauhan Publishing,
[2017] | Includes bibliographical references and index.
Identifiers: LCCN 2017033041 (print) | LCCN 2017035975 (ebook) |
ISBN 9780872332515 (ebook) | ISBN 9780872332508 (pbk. : alk. paper)
Subjects: LCSH: Hancock (N.H.)–Anecdotes. | Hancock (N.H.)–
Social life and customs. | City and town life--New Hampshire.
Classification: LCC F44.H4 (ebook) | LCC F44.H4 M36 2017 (print) |
DDC 974.2/8–dc23
LC record available at https://lccn.loc.gov/2017033041

Book design by Sarah Bauhan
Text set in Michael Harvey's Mentor Pro and Strayhorn
Cover design by Henry James
Printed by Versa Press

BAUHAN PUBLISHING LLC
44 MAIN STREET PETERBOROUGH NEW HAMPSHIRE 03458
603-567-4430
WWW.BAUHANPUBLISHING.COM
sales@bauhanpublishing.com

To contact Howard Mansfield:
www.howardmansfield.com

ONCE AGAIN, AND ALWAYS,
FOR DR. B. A. MILLMOSS

CONTENTS

༕༖༕

SMALL TOWNS, LARGE QUESTIONS

On a few acres in my town, scientists are listening deep into space, sifting the static, trying to find the origin and the end of the universe. The big white dish of the radio antenna has the presence of a question mark.

Just down the road from the observatory, Thornton Wilder wrote *Our Town* more than seventy-five years ago, when the universe as we knew it was a smaller place but the questions we all ask were just as large.

At the end of Act I, Rebecca Gibbs tells her brother George how the minister addresses a letter: "It said: Jane Crofut; The Crofut Farm; Grover's Corners; Sutton County; New Hampshire; United States of America; Continent of North America; Western Hemisphere; the Earth; the Solar System; the Universe; the Mind of God—that's what it said on the envelope. . . . And the postman brought it just the same."

The New England village, Grover's Corners, was nested securely in a series of ever larger spheres.

In modern cosmology, the universe dances. Nothing is fixed. Time bends. The short story of our settlement here in America tells a similar story: it's a constant nervous migration. Many of the villages we praise have been on the move most of their lives.

Open almost any guidebook or history of New England written in the last 250 years and you will find the village praised as "one of the most delightful prospects which this world can afford," as Yale president Timothy Dwight wrote of his travels in the 1790s. A place possessing the fitness and poise of a clipper ship, "the highest and choicest beauty," as the great landscape architect Frederick Law Olmsted said in the late nineteenth century.

Such praise casts the village as a beauty-pageant winner, all dressed up with no place to go. The village is seen as a finished work. But these villages, like all American places, are fluid, mercurial. Some were settled first on a hill, then moved down by the water to run the mills. When the railroad came, they followed the rails, and when the automobile came to rule, they slopped across the landscape in malls, condos, and food joints. At its debut in 1935, *Yankee* magazine lamented a New England "about to be sold, to be 'swallered inter' a sea of chain stores, national releases, and nationwide hookups."

Some towns were a small Pleiades, a cluster of a half-dozen little villages, which was soon eclipsed by a growing central village, which itself burned brightly until the auto age.

Other villages are the story of the rise and fall of one commodity: clothespins, shoes, rocking chairs, buggy whips. American places are often but a rumor of community wrapped around the commerce of the moment. Walk a few rods into the woods around here and you will find the cellar holes of farms and small villages that long ago failed.

To the many villages pursuing a revival, this history is like the old joke: The bad news is that these villages have changed, and the good news is that they can change again. We are a restless people, suckers for those magazine lists of the "Best Ten Towns to Live in This Week." "The lesson is this," advised one real estate wizard. "When migration turns to a new region, do not clutch the dying past. Let go and move on." We don't settle a place as much as we experiment with it.

Some towns are as imperiled as the family farm, as sitting down to dinner together with the family—with no appliances talking at you. Many beautiful, important places are being lost; a few will be saved. In your lifetime you have likely seen small towns crumble like sand castles on the beach.

Tremendous forces are working against small communities. These have been well documented: the car, the TV, the net, the automatic teller machine, the entire growing electronic cocoon. We are more invisible to one another. Our inventions have atomizing effects and reinforce isolation. They celebrate individualism and starve the commons.

Every public policy we have set in motion since World War II works against the town: the model zoning codes, the funding and building of highways, the post office's eagerness to move from town centers. We have built a machine to create sprawl and it is wickedly successful. We have taken our penchant for migration and magnified it a hundredfold. We love our cars and our roads more than our public places.

Against these odds, people are working to save small towns using innovative approaches like community loan funds, land banks, stewardship programs, and old-fashioned volunteerism with long committee hours. They are trying to stop sprawl and find a better way to build. Part of that bad news/good news joke is about newcomers in town: Yes, they don't know the stories and old ways, but they also don't know that things *can't* be done. Often, in partnership with the oldest residents, they take on the toughest challenges.

They see that the grace the guidebooks have spoken of is still there. Time and again they say: I lived out west, down south, etc.—but when I came here, I felt as though I were coming home. I felt as though I had always lived here.

Even after this long anti-village era, the order and repose of many villages has survived. These villages are a story about that most un-American attribute: limits. They are built of a few simple materials, gathered in an ensemble about the streets and commons. Seen from afar, the New England landscape presents a harmonious prospect of village, farm, and forest, another set of nested spheres.

From the top of one of our blueberry hills (which we pridefully call mountains) you can see the white spire of the meetinghouse and the main street of the village, and at times you can see the big white dish poking up among the trees, moving on its quest. *The Universe. The Mind of God.*

That's how we live these days. A small town riding in a universe expanding, racing away from the first moment of time, the Big Bang, to—what?

The astronomers have their questions and we have ours. Will these towns survive? The answers from both searches will be big news.

A MAIN STREET STORY

I have known Hancock's Main Street for about thirty years, going up and down it almost daily, in and out of the library, store, post office, meetinghouse, vestry, and various houses, all of which are on the National Register of Historic Places. A good street is a good narrative—it leads you someplace. And this street will lead you from the foot of Norway Hill to the common and Norway Pond. From the meetinghouse you can look out on the common, the town's oldest burial ground, and Skatutakee Mountain. And yet Main Street has more to offer than these pretty views. It took me a few years to really see the street.

Because we are used to the mandated regularity of modern developments, we tend to expect that the houses would be lined up like soldiers on a parade ground, facing the street precisely.

But when you look, you see that things are a little askew, the houses turned a bit this way and that. Some houses almost hug their neighbors, and others stand apart, aloof. On one side of the street the houses are angled to face south. There is no uniform separation.

Main Street has a finely modulated haphazardness, a gentle dynamism that I've come to think of as asymmetry within symmetry. The street establishes an easily read rhythm and then surprises us with its variations.

Part of this asymmetry comes from the size of the houses. The biggest house is next door to one of the smallest. There's a great variation in size among all the houses, allowing for older families to downsize just by moving next door. This is often forbidden by modern zoning. In a basic subdivision, all the houses are the same size, set back the same distance on similar-size lots.

Main Street's edges are also askew—grass in some places, granite curbing in most places. It still has aspects of the old "soft" landscape—paths formed by foot and hoof. There's a beloved "cowpath" on the south side, a wide path on the other side of the street, and two places with short runs of cement sidewalk. It's also dark at night, which is another survival of the old soft landscape. You can see the Milky Way from Main Street.

One aspect has eroded: there are fewer fences. There were once many unique white fences, erected back when cattle and sheep were driven through the street. The fences that remain are a key part of the street's integrity. Hancock would benefit from a few restored fences, and some more trees to replace the old maples that have been lost.

Main Street is disorderly within limits. It's like town meeting—a roomful of opinionated individuals reaching consensus.

This casual order is not only beautiful, but it is mostly all right. That may seem to be faint praise, but building a new place that is mostly all right is something we have a very hard time doing. Look at any modern street, office park, or even at the serious attempts by the New Urbanists to apply the lessons of a street like this. The new towns they build are frequently dissatisfying; they feel contrived and uptight.

Back in the tear-'em-down era of Urban Renewal, architect Robert Venturi got his colleagues' attention by asking "Is not Main Street almost all right?"

It's the "almost" that's important—it's the "almost" that provides the breathing space. If Main Street were perfect it would be dull; it wouldn't engage us.

Hancock's Main Street isn't a quaint postcard. It's a breathing lesson.

THIS OLD CHAIR

W hen you buy an old place with a barn and a shed or two, you often inherit stray bits of the old life–hints about the history of the house you now call your own. Our small house, barn, and "chicken shack"–a studio that once housed chickens devoted to their own art–came with a small trove of cast-off shutters, old windows, and various hunks of plows, sleds, harnesses, and shoes from the age of the horse and the ox.

My favorite cast-off is a Queen Anne-style dining room chair, which I'm sitting in as I write this. Furniture made during Queen Anne's reign at the start of the eighteenth century is graceful and delicately carved. Its "solid self-assurance . . . is also shown in that two-thirds of an expensive piece of imported wood could be wasted in making the elegant, double-curved cabriole (leg)," says a guide published by the British National Trust.

My much-later New Hampshire translation of this style is self-assured, too, but it's not elegant. It was made by people who knew the heft of a good ax, the feel of a good wooden pail. It was made by workers with a sure sense of practicality. No Yankee is going to waste wood and he's not going to show off whittling it to thinness. A chair should be serious about support; it should offer good value. It should be built like a barn.

This country edition is like a formal gown made from denim instead of silk. It's more Cousin Anne than Queen Anne. The legs have a hint of a curve, but they are rather fat—they are good legs for farm work. The front legs drop straight at the knee, and curve to a wide ankle. The "fiddleback splat"—the central part of the chair back—is hefty. The top rail of the chair overhangs the fiddleback splat and the stiles on the side, so that it looks like a thick, oaken deli sandwich.

This chair was made about twenty-five miles down the road in Keene sometime between World War I and the early years of the Great Depression. A yellowed paper label still hanging on under the seat says Norwood, Calef & Co. The "style number" is penciled in: 3325.

It was probably sold in a set of four, six, or even eight to a striving town merchant or a successful farmer. The Cousin Anne style is a country mouse's reach for the city styles shown in the magazines and movies: *Look at us! Everything's up to date here, too.*

My orphaned chair has had a hard later life, really one

more like barns, which are freely altered for the task at hand. Barns are like workbenches marked by many jobs. The seat was reupholstered in a reddish-brown fake leather. Someone then stood on it to reach a ceiling he or she was painting with a roller—the faux leather is speckled with white paint so that the seat looks like a starry night. The chair back has smudges of white and gray paint, perhaps from one of the artists who used to rent the "chicken shack" studio. But its roughest use came from its short life as a workbench. The fiddleback splat is now only a half a splat; one splintered side goes straight down. Several holes have also been drilled into it.

This has only brought the chair closer to the true character of New Hampshire, a land that is hard used, but resilient. This chair is like many milltowns and their abandoned mills. Thousands upon thousands of days of honest labor have passed by without a memorial. This orphaned chair is a small marker of an honesty that overwhelmed its fancy English heritage. It aspired to a citified elegance, but it has acquired a rougher kind of beauty, like a wrinkled face.

Chairs like this are piled up forgotten in attics, barns, and sheds. They slosh around country auctions. They are sold—if at all—in large lots often at the auction's end and they move on to other auctions, barns, and attics. They are like the Old Man of the Mountain in its last days, when the Great Profile was held together with cables and epoxy. Scars, collapse, and renewal are all part of the New Hampshire landscape. Much of New Hampshire is postcard pretty, but there's much that is rougher. You have to live with it to really see it. It has a kind of grace that's hidden, like a broken, paint-splattered old chair.

FOURTH OF JULY

On July Fourth, I watched the Hancock fireworks show with two people whose memories span the century. We had all gathered for a party on Gordon Laing's lawn. His house looks across Norway Pond toward the main street and the meetinghouse. The volunteer fire department runs the show over the pond.

The day had been rainy, but cleared on toward twilight. A beautiful orange moon rose just to the left of the meetinghouse spire. On the beach you could see a small crowd of fifty or so gathering with, here and there, a flash of the bright green of those night-glow toys. Up the slope, near the carriage shed, was another small group. One canoe was out on the pond. Mist clung to the other end of the pond.

When the fireworks began, my wife had wandered off. I was sitting next to George Kendall. He was the director of the MacDowell Colony from 1952 to 1971. Mr. Kendall—that is how I usually address him—is sharp, polite, and carries a bearing from another time, a quiet but majestic courtliness, all present in small gestures and a solidity of character.

As the first fireworks began, we realized that they were blocked by an old maple tree across the road. Looking through the leaves we could see flashes of the design.

The obscured fireworks were alluring, like a woman's veiled face. Mr. Kendall said that the tree gave the scene a nice country feeling, and I figured that after ninety-odd years, he'd seen enough fireworks. The bright red falling sparks and the dancing blue points of light between the leaves did have a calming effect.

When my wife returned, Mr. Kendall graciously insisted that I go sit with her. I excused myself and we sat down next to Joan Kunhardt, who is ninety and now legally blind.

After the finale—*boom-boom-boom*—short punches of sound and light puncturing the sky—all was quiet. People cheered and applauded all around Norway Pond.

We asked Joan what she thought of the show. "I'm a bad one to ask about fireworks."

"Why?" We thought she'd say something about her sight.

"I remember the armistice, the end of the war in 1918. We had fires out in the street and fireworks. All the men home from the front, when they heard the fireworks, they left. They went home."

"Was this in London?" I asked.

"We lived in Hull, in Humberside. We had been bombed by Zeppelins."

"Did you see it?"

"I saw one go down in flames. I was nine years old. At the start we didn't have any guns to shoot them down, but in the end we did.

"So this—the fireworks—reminds me of World War I. Didn't you think the last ones were too loud? Didn't they hurt your ears?"

We told her how amazed we were by her story.

"It's just where you are in life," she said. "What happens to you."

After the show, Al Lambert took her by the arm and walked her home through the mist and the smoke that often gathers after fireworks.

We went home. Joan's story had given a little fireworks display over a pond a resonance. I couldn't sleep and idly turned on the television. There was a documentary about the baseball of the 1930s and 1950s, a different America when the players came to the park on the subway and were mostly farm boys.

Fourth of July—the intersection of so many pasts: armistice, World War II, and nine-year-olds seeing only the show of one summer's night. So here's to Jefferson and DiMaggio, Joan Kunhardt and the Allies. Here's to all the hidden memories and thoughts in people as they sit silently watching fireworks, veiled by all that color and light.

MY WINTER IN POLITICS

For one winter I was a politician. My blind ambition was to capture one of the glittering prizes of the republic, to be part of the power and the glory. I was running for library trustee in a town of 1,500. Candidates almost always run unopposed for these positions throughout New England. The election is a formality. Or so I was assured when I was asked to serve. I hadn't campaigned for office since a closely contested junior high school race for homeroom rep (I lost) and I wasn't about to start. After I had filed to run, an opponent came forward to stop what some old timers saw as an insurgency of young know-nothings. I was caught up in what the local press pronounced "a heated race." ("You have an opponent?" asked a friend who lives in the city. "You have long winters up there.")

I was hoping to acquit myself with a respectable loss.

My opponent had lived in town since the Year One, and had served on enough committees to merit the Legion d' Honneur. I had already been dismissed from the campaign by my opponent's friend, who had put him up to this. "Nothing personal," he said, "you're a young man, your day will come. . . ." I politely thanked him for calling, and wisely left much unsaid.

The campaign was fought over that hot-button issue: children's story hour. The elementary school up the street sent all students to the library to take out books. The younger students were read stories.

My opponent was against children's story hour. At least he had said something that was reported that way all over town. He had managed to manufacture controversy. Part of the electorate was up in arms.

As each report came back to me, I silently displayed shock and dismay. My eyebrows raised, my jaw dropped. Each time I received the news as if it was fresh, but never did I join in.

So when I'd get my mail in town, there was scarcely a day when I wasn't stopped by someone who would say, indignantly, "Did you hear what he said?"

I'd shake my head no.

"He's against children's story hour!"

Horror—sheer abject horror—would show on my face.

O imperiled ship of state! my face would say. (I have expressive eyebrows.)

It doesn't take a Beltway pollster to tell you that attacking children's story hour is going to pull high negative numbers. *Goodnight Moon*, goodnight candidate.

For the record, as it was reported to me, he didn't say he was against story hour, only that it was useless. "At least the kids get some fresh air walking up the street" is what he may have said.

I never said one bad word about my opponent. In fact, I never said anything about him—a sure way to avoid being misquoted. As his statements piled up I quietly staked out the high ground, and hid. My opponent was doing just fine for the both of us.

I avoided the village store. Anything said at the meat counter is as good as published. I wasn't running for office. In the British tradition, I *stood* for election. It would have been too easy for my opponent to cast me as a young flatlander charging in here to run their lives. This is sometimes stated as: "These flatlanders come up here and think they have to tell us when to come in out of the rain." I'd lived in New Hampshire eight years at the time, and while I did wonder why so many people were soaking wet, that was their business.

He soon topped himself. When he was asked why he wanted to be a trustee, he said, "to keep an eye on the girls at the library," meaning the librarians and the other trustees. I could have mapped the route of that comment as it made a lightning circuit around town. He'd pushed the button of many forthright, independent, hard-working women. Bless him.

He was my campaign's best asset. People in town rallied. They wrote letters to the newspaper, made phone calls. They circulated an election-eve postcard in my support. (Alas, it was printed in red ink. No one but me was appalled at that symbolism.)

The less I said, the better things went. If I won, I would top William McKinley's front porch campaign of 1896. His opponent, William Jennings Bryan, pounded across the country, logging thousands of hard railroad miles. McKinley stayed home. He stood by his ill wife, speaking to visitors from his front porch.

My opponent was campaigning hard, calling everyone in town like some fool flatlander who thinks he has to tell people when to come in out of the rain. I was urged to make myself better known, to call people, to have little teas, but I stuck by the lessons of 1896.

The polling data, such as it was in a small town, was looking favorable: the library volunteers were mine. I detected erosion in his support at the historical society. The women's club and the fire department were showing signs of strong support. The all-important meat counter poll showed me winning an upset victory, as did the checkout counter up front. I was even further ahead in the post office poll. (Never mind that these "polls" count the same few people over and over.)

I won, trouncing my opponent by a margin of nearly three to one (327 enlightened citizens to 140 benighted). The world was made safe for children's story hour. The country went on to seven years of unprecedented economic expansion. And you can thank one small-town library trustee who had the courage to stand up and keep his mouth shut.

THE SKEEZIX CHRONICLES

*(An apology to my neighbor for
foundering on a rock in his pasture.)*

Skeezix arrived already an old man. He was an orphan
from a good home.

Skeezix is a Ford 9N tractor built in 1941. He had known
only one family until recently when our neighbor, Dick
Amidon, had to go to a nursing home and my wife thought
that a tractor to mow our pasture was just a perfect surprise
birthday present. I viewed it warily. Here was another ma-
chine with its own schedule of machine needs. I named
the tractor Skeezix after an orphan in an old comic strip,
Gasoline Alley, which was our neighbor's favorite.

The 9N, an antique that debuted in 1939 and is still
working on thousands of small holdings, is an elemental
machine dressed in a serious battleship gray. It looks like

a black and white photo of itself, as if it had rolled out of a Walker Evans Depression-era photo. The slim owner's manual assumes a level of machine knowledge once common for farmers, millhands, and an America always tinkering and flooding the patent office with improved ways of doing everything. The manual is like those old cookbooks that begin by instructing, "First, make a roux."

To operate a 9N is to step back to our machine past, to a time before cars had power steering, power brakes, and automatic transmissions, before cars got so easy to drive that some people busy themselves texting. The tractor requires your entire attention and you train your ear to its every sound, to the whirring of the PTO—Power Take Off—that drives the mower or thresher, and to the engine speed, which is controlled by a throttle on the steering column. There's no drifting along dreamily plugged into your iPod.

Actually, this antique was a revolutionary machine that transformed the tractor from a mere mechanical horse pulling plows and harrows to one that powered those tools, and hundreds of others, via an ingenious hydraulic hitch-and-lift system invented by Harry Ferguson. With this hitch, say tractor historians, all agriculture changed. All tractors since are heirs to the Ford 9N.

Ford's later tractors, like the 8N from 1947, which is painted a cheery red and a more welcoming lighter gray, had numerous improvements. I won't bother you with these, except to say that after living with 1939's breakthrough technology, I'm envious of the modern machine

comforts of 1947. (Among them, the ability to simultaneous-
ly step on the brakes and the clutch. With the 9N you can
choose: the brake for one rear wheel and the clutch. The
8N put both brake pedals next to each other. Nice, since
there are few three-legged farmers.)

Mowing our small field—about three acres—I learned
how to turn without having the lightly weighted front
wheel skate past the corner, and to ease into reverse, which
is geared so high that it shoots you back with a crazy jolt, as
if driven by a leadfoot teen. And I learned that my brakes
needed adjustment; I had to stomp on them. The Ford trac-
tors were advertised as being easy enough for a ten-year-old
farm girl to run. Either those farm girls were built like line-
backers destined to lead Ohio State to the Rose Bowl, or my
brakes pedals were too stiff.

With hours of experience in a field where I knew every
rock, dip, and twist, I was emboldened to cross the road and
mow my neighbors' field as a surprise. They were away for
a few weeks. Hunt and Sara Dowse had recently increased
their holdings, buying Skeezix's old field from our neigh-
bor. This would be a homecoming, and if Skeezix were a
horse, I could have just let him lead the way.

I walked the field several times, noting the rocks and
wet places, planning my route. I was a little iffy about one
area among some trees, but otherwise things looked good.

Off I went at the madcap speed of two miles per hour,
maybe three miles per hour at times. I was going along
fine. On about my fifth revolution of the field—up by those

trees—I struck a rock. Square on. I never saw the rock until I was riding up over it, trying to stop. This is not a good feeling. The sheep, who visit each year, had eaten little of the grass here. The rock was hiding in the tall grass.

Poor Skeezix was hung up on a rock as tall as a tombstone. It was definitive; there was no way of wriggling the tractor free. I turned off the tractor and surrendered my standing as A Guy Who Knows About Stuff. I called another neighbor, a guy who really does know about stuff and who operated construction cranes on skyscrapers. He used the bucket loader on his (modern) tractor to lift the old Ford off the rock. He wasn't much concerned. This kind of thing happens, he said generously.

Once the tractor was free, I saw that the rock was drenched with what turned out to be transmission fluid. Nothing appeared to be bent on the tractor, but it was leaking fluid and I could no longer lift the mowing deck.

A further surrender followed. I gave up on the surprise and emailed my blissfully unaware vacationing neighbors Hunt and Sara, confessing to the accident and concluding the tale: "So: Welcome home! Surprise! What a wonderful neighbor you have! I mowed about 20 percent* of your field—and now I need your help getting the tractor going again. (*OK, maybe 10 percent. I was never good at fractions.)"

Fortunately Hunt is part of what I call the Model T Brain Trust. He restores Model Ts, as does another neighbor, Wayne Fisher. The third member of the Trust, Bud Wilder, is retired from running the garage in town. On

Hunt's return, they diagnosed the problem—I had shattered a drain plug for the transmission—and they began opening drawers in Hunt's workshop and spilling out small piles of bolts. They loved the challenge. I stood by like an early aviator who's been shot down, in this case by my own ineptitude. They then scattered to two other workshops and fabricated a new drain plug by cutting apart and joining different old bolts.

I did finish mowing the field and I offered to mow it again the next year. Hunt silently demurred. That's a favor he can live without. I don't think Skeezix will be crossing the road again.

SIGNS AND NUMBERS

In my town, we have exchanged storytelling for signs and numbers. All the roads now have small green and white signs, like name tags at a conference. Once there were no signs on these roads—one half of them dirt—and no house numbers.

Directions, whether given to visitors or the FedEx courier, usually partook of town history and geography, prominent rocks and families each receiving a mention. To get your package delivered, you'd go through a roster of the families who had lived in your house and the neighboring houses. The delivery person often added the history he knew. (Which is how we learned that years ago the plaster ceiling in our living room had fallen in.) If you lived near a famous rock (like the Elephant Rock), all the better. I have seen these little narratives jammed onto the computer forms where it says "address."

You could talk your way back to a laundry day in 1789, if you wanted. But ordinarily things went no deeper than the 1930s—and this in the course of directions.

Stories sometimes meander. They mean different things to different people in different tellings. When you asked someone for directions, you really said: Tell me a story. A story about lives and landscapes and maybe how the weather was. Not a bad start to a trip. Not a bad map to life.

But a bad way to send out a fire engine or an ambulance. All across New Hampshire, towns have had to label and sometimes rename their roads as we converted to a 9-1-1 emergency dispatch system. So now we have numbers—three-and-a-half inches tall, reflective, and posted in the prescribed manner.

There was reticence the old way. Why go blabbing your name to every damn fool who passes by? It smacks of advertising. These new signs might as well say "Hi! My name is Orchard Road! Help yourself to a drink—Coke, beer, over there!"

Admittedly, it was confusing without street signs. Old Antrim Road had, like some strand of DNA, split and replicated itself a few times so that it was four or more separate roads, and seemed to be running off everywhere, toward Antrim, New Hampshire, and the county Antrim in Ireland.

So many roads, like cats, had two or more names. In Hancock, Main Street was also known as Forest Road, Stoddard Road, and Route 123. Jaquith Road was also Eastview, Harrisville, and Nelson Road. It depended on where you were going. Why should it be the same road in both directions? It's a different road coming and going. The old rural landscape was a larger place than today's paved world.

Who knew, really, where Bond's Corner Road became Sand Hill Road? This was a philosophical question about where one was and where one was headed. The many names of the old roads were like the starched preachers of the old upright New England, asking: And just what is your purpose on this journey? A road marked Route 137 poses no questions, no dilemmas; it's all about access and speed.

Many towns faced a big housecleaning to sweep away old names. Walpole and North Walpole had fifteen identical names between them, including an emotionally contested Main Street. (North Walpole claimed they had a Main Street first. Its sister village was a Johnny-come-lately, grabbing the name only recently, in 1862.)

New Ipswich had a tangle so complicated it took a computer software designer with a PhD from MIT, Jeff MacGillivray, to sort it out. (He also has a sense of humor and, important in those get-off-my-land face-offs, a big stride.) "Basically," he says, "you need an organizing mind, a willingness to listen, and a flak jacket."

About one quarter of New Ipswich's roads had multiple names. The extreme case was a one-hundred-foot-long road in the far north of town with three names, including South Road. In one place Old Tenney Road divided itself into two Old Tenney Roads. You could be at the intersection of Old Tenney, Old Tenney, and Old Tenney (which was not to be confused with yet another Old Tenney Road three miles away). Many times MacGillivray faced neighbors who thought they were living on different roads: Old County Road, County Road, Old *Country* Road, and Academy Road. All this in a quarter of a mile.

The selectmen honored MacGillivray, and while he's not in need of work, I have his next assignment: London. I count in my copy of *London A–Z* (pronounced A to *Zed*, and don't cross the ocean without it): twenty-two Kings (or King's) Roads, twelve Kings (or King's) Avenues, eleven King Streets, forty-six High Streets, more than forty Park Roads, nearly seventy Victoria Roads, Avenues, Streets, Terraces, Crescents, and Embankments. . . .

Many streets in London change their names every few blocks, as if to prove what the writer André Gide once said: "Please don't understand me too quickly." With our new signs and numbers, the world is more fixed, more known, and as the old names fall away, less understood.

ON GOING LATE TO YARD SALES

E veryone will tell you to go early to a yard sale, but I recommend going late. You won't come home with many treasures, but you will walk away with a glimpse of the riddles that are other people's lives.

In the last hour of a yard sale, the sellers are exhausted. They may be remorseful about what has sold and what remains. They have a look of soporific regret, much like the dullness that follows gluttony. They are not cleansed by losing some useless things. Rather, they seem exposed, as if their junk—old chairs and blenders—was off with the new owners telling secrets on them. They have put part of themselves in boxes out on the driveway, and watched themselves scatter to the winds. They are surprised. They had just put stuff out to sell and now they feel diminished and judged. Late at yard sales, they sit trying to decipher the verdict.

Here are the "object-secrets" of a house outside in the sunshine, the intimate now public. They still retain a touch of their domestic duty, the marks of wear and use. Once they were commodities, one of a million produced in a factory, then they were possessions, and now at a yard sale they are a third thing, existing in uncertainty. Some of these things are on the cusp of being trash; some have gained value as a fetish, a prized collectible.

What we are seeing at yard sales are moments of uncertainty. It's as if the driveway or barn or garage sat on a seesaw. Are we witnessing the end of an empire, the breakup of a marriage? Is someone decamping for another dream-vector, another fate-center on the map? Is the rest of the seller's life as bereft of grace as this driveway selection?

I remember two houses in particular. Each yard sale marked an ending, one happy, one not.

At the happy place, my wife and I arrived after the owners had nothing left to sell. It was an old farm and the couple was in their late sixties. We got to chatting: their family had raised chickens, goats, sheep, horses. . . . They'd done it all, and now they were moving on. They had come to New Hampshire in the 1950s, after the Korean War, and it had been a good life, the woman told us, and she smiled as she said this. She had the poise not to be disappointed by her yard sale; she could let go.

The unhappy house was easy to spot. It was a house divided—half of it painted a chocolate-bar brown, the other half a thin, sloppy white, like skim milk. The line where brown met white was rough and ran from the foundation to the eaves.

At the sale only a few heavy objects were left, including a dubious avocado-green refrigerator and an air-hockey table that weighed more than our car. A man and a woman (husband and wife?) sat there, silently, in different spheres.

We edged quietly back to our car. The house was sour with old anger.

"What do you think happened there?" my wife asked.

"Kaboom," I mimed, moving my hands wide apart.

If you go early to a yard sale, pushing in during the Oklahoma-land-rush frenzy, you may find some bargains, but you will miss the puzzles that are left when the boxes are nearly empty.

THE ASK

I was long an adult before someone sat me down and told me the facts of The Ask. I was serving on a small board and we'd called in a fundraiser we all knew for advice. She told us that a record amount of wealth is going to change hands in the next thirty years. She gave us a figure. It was some whopping big number, something like $30 trillion. We were surprised. We had never thought about it. Money was just what some people had. But as she showed us, money was a river, pooling here or there for a generation or two, before moving on. There are fundraisers making calls all over town, she said. People from Harvard, Dartmouth, Brown, Smith, and other universities and many charities are calling, making "The Ask."

"The what?" we innocents said. "The Ask." We'd never heard of that either. She explained that you don't just ask someone for money. It's a nuanced dance. The Ask is a careful consideration of who goes to ask for money, how they ask, what they ask for, and when they ask. It's cloaked by informality—*oh, yes, please stop by*—but it's about as formal as American life gets outside of taking an oath of office.

Each party knows the reason for the visit. Each has a number in mind—zero may be one of the numbers—but that comes in its time. Money is the rude fact that is evaded until the proper moment.

All of this was news to us. In small towns, and society in general, we live by the Don't Ask. We let our neighbors pursue their lives, in happiness or sorrow. We don't interfere; we don't snoop. We ask each other for time, respect, patience, understanding, visibility, and invisibility. *Look at us, look away.* Invisibility is essential. We avert our gaze. We mute our curiosity. We give our neighbors the room to live. We don't question their contradictions. When I was younger I would have called this hypocrisy. Now I think it may be kindness, or just the mercy we show each other. It is, however, tangled up in false telling, and you have to refuse a numb acceptance of cruelty and suffering.

Inside the Don't Ask is the concealed kernel of The Ask. Almost all of the asking in small-town life is implied: We're neighbors; we're in this together. Of course you'll show up, volunteer, help out. Sometimes it is an outright Ask: Will you vote for this, serve on the committee, help run the tag sale? But usually it's indirect, a look, a pause, a question that isn't really a question, but underlies what you're supposed to know. Polite society is an avenue of exits so we don't have to directly say "no." (Societies differ in these forms of evasion. It's what trips up tourists time and again.) Community life is about how much we ask of each other, and how we ask it. Often what we ask of each other is that we don't ask.

The Ask cruises the line, breaks the rule of Don't Ask. The Ask is one of the few places where you see adults learning rules of conduct as if they were in the second grade. All the pep talks and PowerPoint slides by the fundraising coaches remind me of some elementary school teacher telling you about washing your hands and sharing toys.

The formal Ask breaks the code of not asking, and it does so with a scripted ritual. There is an actual script, a prescribed way to ask. Once you're talking money, the script is a good railing to hold. Talking money with your neighbor is otherwise taboo.

There are rules, or as one guru of The Ask says, there are steps. Think of it as stairs and you go up one step at a time. You make sure you know all about your quarry (the potential donor). You have some idea of his or her "capacity," how much they've given in the past and what they might give now. You call first. You make sure that a person with the right prestige is asking. You don't insult your quarry by asking for too little or too much.

You may ask on the first visit, but big donations usually require a number of visits. The first visit isn't about money—

"I'm not going to ask you for a gift today," you are supposed to say as a way of putting your quarry at ease—but you have to ask them for a follow-up meeting. It's a courtship; few people go from hello to the altar in one conversation.

After some small talk you look for the moment to "transition" to the reason for your visit. When you make your pitch, you don't pitch. You show your commitment to the cause, vividly state the case, "make them cry," as one fundraiser says, but you're not selling them. You're trying to "partner with them" and help them "meet their philanthropic objectives," or some such talk that is cloaked in Rotary Club breakfast optimism: You're giving *them* a chance to support something they believe in. How good of you.

It's a ceremonial visit that says I wouldn't cross this line of Don't Ask if I didn't already know that we agree on this request, this cause. Let me help you find the best way to donate. This is close to the car dealer who says, "What would it take to put you in this car today? Let's work together."

And finally, after no more than a half hour, you ask for a specific amount of money. This is the moment of doubt—should I ask for less, for more? And it is the moment when after all the letters, emails, phone calls, and chitchat, you are actually talking about money. You've made the grand procession up to the temple mount, stopped to make offerings at the shrines of the lesser gods, and now you are in the temple at the altar. In some scripts you don't come right out and ask, but hand them a chart showing the "pyramid of gifts" as you say, "We're looking for ten gifts of $50,000, fifteen of $25,000," and indicate where on the pyramid they might be (as if we were Victorians too shy to mention a bodily function). Other scripts prompt you to be direct: "We'd like you to consider," "could you contribute," or even the more brazen, "I want you to donate X amount."

You ask and then you shut up. Silence. The subject of money is in the room. You don't want to talk yourself out of the money. Some advisors suggest asking for a glass of water ahead of time so you can wait out the silence by taking a long, slow drink.

Here the quarry will say yes, or let me think about it, or: no. And why no?—you have to ask. It's one of three reasons: this cause isn't important; you're asking for too much money; or it's not the right time.

If they say no, you're not to take it personally; except that "people give to people," the fundraising professionals say.

So, The Ask is a courtship, it's a climb, it's about a taboo, and it's about asking someone directly for something. Not easy.

The Ask. We should take it as a warning that this verb is a noun. Trendy consultant talk and academic fog converts verbs into nouns. (A cartoon in the *New York Times Opinionator* blog about "those irritating nouns as verbs" shows a writer at his desk. "How to make write," it says as it follows the writer through "the envision, the inspire, the create, the reveal, the revise, the submit. . . .") Perhaps as with Thoreau's warning to be wary of "all enterprises that require new clothes," we should also be wary of any undertaking that has been converted from a verb to a noun.

Many years after being introduced to The Ask, I had to do the asking. I was serving on a committee of a nonprofit organization. (Brother, can you spare a grand?) I learned just how flimsy the script can be. There are many questions in play.

What are we asking for? Money, yes. But also we're asking: Does your vision of the world square with ours? Are we agreed about obligations, civic duty, and all that? Or are you going to blow your wad on flashy cars, big TVs, and a condo in warmer climes? (And if so, are you going to invite us?)

You're asking for money and thus you're asking, indirectly, How much money do you have? And where does your money come from? You don't ask this of course, but you're uncomfortably close to looking in someone's cabinets and drawers, and to asking what they spend their money on.

The Ask is about so much more than a donation; you're asking someone if they have enough—and how they define that. You're asking them to set aside a corner of their field for the less fortunate to come and harvest. You're asking them to admit they have a surplus.

You've come to look into someone's wallet and their

46

heart. You're asking them to forego whatever it is that money means. Money isn't just money, the smart financial advisers know. It's security to some; it's a hedge against dying. It's status, a sign of their worth to themselves and others. It's possibility. It's something new, maybe, a treat, a new car, a trip, a lake house. It may be about pride if they earned it, or guilt if they inherited it.

Old New Englanders adhere to a private/public show of wealth. They want to be respected for their money but you're not to mention it. They carry on the Puritan ethic of downplaying wealth. They make a show of not showing with their inherited, worn Persian rugs, beat up cars, shambling colonial capes, and conversations sprinkled with the right prep schools, colleges, clubs, and summer retreats. Money is kept in the background, but it is king. Money is the gravity by which they control every gesture around them.

To ask someone for money is to open a door on a poorly lit room. You don't know what you may find and it takes your eyes a while to adjust. This is one of the last taboos. It isn't as intrusive as doing some sort of town-wide sex survey, but it is awfully close.

So it was that I found myself in deep, intimate discussions about job security, family illness, and errant grandchildren. As I sat back in the chair, I could only nod and think, "Well, I asked."

If your visit goes well, everyone can marinate in their own civic virtue. If it goes poorly, it's like stubbing your toe, or curling–that game where you sweep a round stone down the ice–but you don't have the ice. You're left with a polite back and forth that may get thicker as your conversation continues.

ᐅᐅᐅ

On a winter night when it was hovering near zero, with the snow banked high and the stars etched in the black, Alex and I went to call on Bill to seek a donation for our worthy nonprofit. I arrived first. I saw him sitting in a wingback chair by the window. He wasn't reading a book, or watching the news, though I suppose he could have been doing either moments before.

He looked resigned, pensive. I wasn't sure, but for a guy in a comfy wingback chair he looked sea-tossed. I came in and took off my heaviest coat, hat, gloves, and tried to shake off the cold. We chatted until Alex got there. Alex is a surgeon who has the calm manner you'd want in someone who cuts into people for a living.

Alex arrived and we began our spiel about the nonprofit's mission, how well it was doing, and of course, how, with Bill's help, it could do more. I sensed a distance in Bill that I had not seen before, a resistance. He seemed far away. After a while I was unsure of how to proceed, but Alex, with his sunny nature and level doctor's manner, pressed on and we got a vague assent to $5,000, with an agreement to look at $10,000.

But during that last phase Bill told us that his wife had Alzheimer's. The air in the room thickened, almost as if it were jelling. We told him that we were sorry. He said that no one in town knew and that anyway this didn't affect what we're talking about it. But it did.

We were silent. Somewhere a clock—a regulator or a grandfather clock—ticked, ticked through the quiet, giving the silence dimension.

We asked more about her. It had been coming on for a year, he said. A few months ago he had quit his job at a prestigious law firm. He loved that job. Even though he was a decade past the retirement age, he was at work by 6:30 a.m. every day. But his wife, who had been busy her whole life, asked him to quit—she felt lonely; she didn't know how to spend her days.

Just this week they'd seen the doctor and the psychiatrist for a test. Fortunately they have long-term care insurance, he said. He said something about "things keep changing" and mentioned a grandson's college tuition and a stock that had done well for him.

There we were, three men in a quiet house in the woods. You'd die if you were outside too long tonight, and you'll die eventually indoors. It felt like end times. Bill, I could see now, was melancholic, depressed. I'd seen him around now and then. I had no idea. This sad old man sitting in a wingback chair.

This was a time when his empire had turned to sand, when what he'd done—raised two sons, looked after grandchildren, built a fine house, lavishly volunteered years of work for his town and church—when all that is like a sandcastle in the tides. It doesn't take a big wave, just the water's rising to dissolve it all. It doesn't really dissolve; his good works are walking in the world. But he may have felt that what he had to show for his work was illness and death.

Silence. Clock ticking. A word or two in the jelled air. Time had once hurried on and now stood here refusing to move. So much time gone by, so many seasons fled.

We had come to ask for money to continue the empire building and ended up uncovering a hidden illness. We ended our visit. We left him in thought, a man adrift in his own living room.

Talking about money—money and obligations, money and doing good—led me into some very private discussions. The Ask is a courtship and courtship can lead to intimacy.

We have many glancing meetings in our lives. We run into people while we're on our way someplace else—Hi. How's it going? we ask, and we're gone. Meteors, errant travelers in the sky. We're living our life, or as the Buddhist instructor said, "life is living itself through us." The next we hear is that the person we just saw has died. And we say the last time I saw her, I was on my way here, she was going there. The last time I saw Walter was at the dump. The last time I saw Mike was at the fish market. Over the years I have interviewed many people, and whenever we get to someone who has recently died, they'll tell me where they last saw him, at the market or at a meeting. I was struck by how mundane it was—but that's just it. Where else do we see each other but in our mundane orbits?

These glancing meetings, these nonmeetings, are a big part of life. We're on our way, on some errand, to do something "important." And there goes life, it goes right by.

HEYWOOD'S GARAGE

J im Heywood is the only mechanic I have ever seen work on a car with a hammer. He used to build racing cars. "We'd cut up a '52 Ford, weld 'em. We'd have ourselves a hell of a time," he says. He raced modified stock cars in the B division, "bombers" they called them. Heywood belongs to the old school of auto mechanics: He is no parts jockey—no out of the box and onto the car. He has welded, snipped, and, yes, hammered his way to repairs better than the original part.

Jim and his wife, Linda, run Heywood's Garage, a small cinderblock building with two garage doors on a dead-end side street in the small mill town of Greenville, New Hampshire. Linda operates the office, keeping impeccable files for each customer—repairs, warranties, birthdays, and wedding photos, all in one folder. I have gone there for years for car repairs and theater. Heywood towed me in and though I've since moved twenty miles away, I'm loyal: I've lost track of how much he's saved me by making do. He may just take out the big hammer for the look on my face (shock and awe). Jim brings to car repair the suspense of improvisational theater.

Heywood's has an extensive cast. Standing around, twisting my foot on a greasy spot, I have heard impassioned monologues about gas mileage, buying American cars, school taxes, hemorrhoids, and the disadvantages of the imperial gallon in Canada, where gas costs twice as much.

"They have a larger gallon," says Mr. Bugbee, a big man who manages to look like a grammar school kid in hand-me-downs because all his clothes are too big.

"The imperial gallon," I say. (I have no idea why I know this.)

"How much more is that?" asks Jim, from under a hood.

"A quart," says Mr. Bugbee. For some reason we call him "mister."

"Not worth it. No way," says Jim.

Mr. Bugbee moves on to the Canadian lottery.

"They have a game up there like the Mass. lottery. I played my numbers. I won $10. I left $30 with my cousin. Told him to play the same numbers. They have a $65 million pay off—$65 *million*—one check." At that Mr. Bugbee rocks back a little to enjoy the thought. He is smiling.

I interrupt his reverie. "What would the taxes be?"

"Well," he says, still smiling, "you wouldn't take it out of

Canada. Right away you lose thirty-six cents on the dollar. And the minute you bring it across the border the feds get their share. You leave it there and just write checks."

He had thought it all through. Why not? He was a lucky man. He'd won $10, why not $65 million? You can't get this range of expertise at Jiffy Lube.

Heywood's Garage sits next to the house where two of his brothers live. Jim grew up in Greenville. Another brother and a sister live in a nearby town. Next to his brothers' house, at the end of the street, Jim's last racecar sits in a small grassy lot, crouching like a stalking cat. It looks like an outline of a car in tubes with four big wheels. His racing days are long past. It just got too expensive to compete.

Jim doesn't talk much about racing, but one day (after I'd been going there for eight years) Linda showed me a photo album they have from the old racing days. In one photo Jim is receiving a trophy. He is all victory, smiling. His head is back, thick hair waving. He looks sweaty and triumphant. Underneath that photo is one of his car in the lead. It's the perfect tableau of victory. In a few news clips about the race, Jim graciously says, "Winning is team work and I owe it to my crew." When I read that aloud, he says, "No kidding, those are the guys that put your tires on." Jim told me about his first race; he was in the lead and looked behind him to see if anyone was gaining. He crashed into the wall. He was fifteen years old, too young for a license for the street. He was brought up on racing. Both his father and his mother raced.

He met Linda at the race track. Her uncle also raced. She grew up in a small town in Massachusetts. Her parents, like his, worked in the mills. Jim and Linda have worked hard to build up Heywood's. For years Jim worked without a lift, the fixture of all garages. He used to jack up cars with a small dolly. He spent a lot of time on the cold floor. In the winter he'd wear a raincoat because of all of the ice falling off the cars. But a dozen years ago he raised the roof, put in a lift and spruced up the whole place. He painted the interior a robin's egg blue, cinderblock by cinderblock. He was up there on a ladder painting for so long that we took to calling him Vincent Van Heywood. He even threw out a good portion of his hoard of rusting pipes and car parts that were stacked like cordwood. Things were getting so fancy that we asked him when the chandelier and oriental rugs were going in.

They still love racing. Each winter Jim and Linda close up shop at the end of January and drive to Florida to watch the races at Daytona.

Their daughter, Gina, threw them a surprise party at the American Legion hall for their twenty-fifth anniversary. One hundred fifty friends, relatives, and customers danced until 2 a.m. They had to pass the hat to pay the band to stay later. "People didn't want to go home," says Linda.

WAR OF THE MULTIFLORA ROSES

For more than twenty years we have been waging the War of the Roses—not the roses representing the two royal houses that fought for the English throne, but the invasive *Rosa multiflora*, an import from Asia that has thrived here. A neighbor, who shall remain nameless because he has done many good works, planted it years ago at the urging of a cooperative extension agent. Starting in the 1930s, the US Soil Conservation Service promoted *Rosa multiflora* to fight erosion, provide cover for game birds, and best of all, to be a "living fence" to control livestock. The rose took off and is now choking out native species in about thirty states. "Its tenacious and unstoppable growth habit was eventually recognized as a problem," says the National Park Service. The average *Rosa multiflora* "may produce a million seeds per year, which may remain viable in the soil for up to twenty years."

This "living fence" has made itself at home all over our land. If we didn't mow and bush hog, it would be pushing up through the floorboards of our house, engulfing furniture. We'd have to bush hog our dining room.

It has the strongest will to live that I have seen up close. Cut it back, and the rose seems to say, "Oh, thank you," and it comes back doubly thick. Dig up its roots—dig all the way to China—and one small bit of root will shoot right up. It doesn't go down without a fight—the thorns on its whip-like branches reach out to scratch you, no matter how well covered you are.

And don't just pile up the cuttings, as we did in our naive first years, because they will take root. We have planted several new bushes this way. (Bushes are a diminutive term for something forty feet long, eight feet tall—and spreading.)

We have waged this war most fervently in our pasture, a couple of acres that are fenced for horses and sheep. In the first years the pasture pretty much took care of itself. Neighbors kept their horses there and mowed at the season's end. But the horses left after two divorces (victims of broken stables), and even though the field was still mowed, a few "rock islands"—bushes and trees growing near large rocks—began to assert themselves. The rose, in particular, has a way of claiming land, leaning out with its thorns so that the tractor driver steers around it. Victorious, the rose sprawls out further. Along the fence, the rose and another invasive, Russian olive, with its needle-like thorns, began to spread. Everything in nature provides an edge for something to thrive. The fence and the rocks were enough "edge" for the rose.

Even though I yearly took away pickup truckloads to the burn pile at the dump, we were losing. The pasture wanted to grow up into thickets of roses and, in no time, enact the entire "old field succession" illustration in the ecology books, returning to forest.

We called in men with big machinery. Brian arrived first and attacked the huge rose "bush" that was like a green tidal wave pushing up and over the fence. It was three or four times larger than his orange tractor. He'd grab at part of the bush, and it would crackle like oil in a frying pan. The bush would resist, and the tractor would rock back, like a boxer hit on his chin. The tractor would prevail, pulling up a huge root that was part alien, part transatlantic cable. He'd drive toward the burn pile with a tangle of bush and root, the tractor holding it aloft like a severed head. Then he'd return and get off his tractor to plan his next move. I'd see him in that sideways golfer's crouch, as if he were asking his caddy which putter to use.

Other machinery followed. We cut dead elms and some snaggly old cherry trees. They were bent and twisted, standing in clumps like Babushka basketball players. We had a guy with an excavator pull out the stumps and dig out more of the rose roots. The excavator was clumsy and strong. It pawed at the earth. When the back of the bucket patted the earth down, it was like an awkward monster love pat, a crude mimic of a dog's paw reaching out to touch you.

As the tree roots came up, I was filled with regret. Even the scrawniest tree trunk is anchored by an underground civilization of roots. It's strong. One sees how tenacious the tree was, how tenacious everything is for life.

The ground was wounded with big dirty patches, a battlefield of torn-up roots, unhoused rocks, and the rumpled scars of tracked-up land. Like any operation to body, earth, or soul, the violence is always more than one bargained for. The wound is a surprise.

The cleared pasture looked naked. Though we had removed only a few gnarly old stands of small trees and the rose thickets, the entire field seemed too empty, as if we'd removed some spirit. It lost a little of its roughshod, old-field qualities.

Keeping a pasture open unites us with one of New Hampshire's older epics: pushing back the forest, what they used to call "making land." We have restored an antique landscape. What may look like only a field when you pass by is really a curated object. It takes dedication to keep a pasture, a hay field, a meadow, open. We have a fine society that looks after the forest in New Hampshire, but as our friend the architect Dan Scully once suggested, we could also use a Society for the Preservation of Open Fields. As we return to growing more of our food locally, these antiques will be in demand.

A SUNDAY IN TOWN

On a sunny weekend, the last of February, all of Hancock seemed to be outdoors, skiing, snowshoeing, ice-fishing, snowmobiling. After a long, snowless winter—an "open winter" of bare ground—it had snowed in the last two weeks. People had come to believe in the snow, believe it is here, and alter their habits. All sorts of equipment had been pulled out of closets and the corners of garages and barns.

We took a short snowshoe hike over to Spoonwood Pond on Saturday. Spoonwood was quiet. A strong headwind on the journey back over the ice made our arrival among the bob houses seem like a return to an arctic village. In front of one bob house sat four or five people, sheltered from the wind, with a fire going. A man overcome with happiness showed us a lake trout he had caught—five pounds, maybe fourteen inches long. Biggest fish I'd ever seen pulled up through the ice. He could scarcely believe it. He'd always told his wife that he'd return with dinner, he said. He just never had. His friend held the gasping fish up by the gills for us to see, as if he were posing for a photo. I couldn't look too long, though, knowing that the fish was suffocating, gasping for water.

ᏣᏣᏣ

On Sunday I played the country vicar and visited with about a dozen people or more in my chase to get a signed letter off to the newspaper. I was running for library trustee, usually an uncontested position, but a gaggle of grouchy men—they call themselves the Old Crocks—was contesting my candidacy. I had to gather about a dozen signatures for one of those tedious letters of support.

Sunday is a domestic day, one day when people are truly at home, and not "on the run." I took the measure of Sundays in many living rooms and kitchens. I was offered gallons of tea and coffee. I sat and chatted. I admired old cats and young cats, views out the window toward ponds, woods, and fields. I looked at new woodwork, and the oldest in town, planks more than a yard wide.

In all the houses it was quiet—no TV, no radio, the Sunday paper out on a table. I was like a missile hurtling through the quiet. I had to see all these folks in a hectic two-hour loop of town.

My campaign started in front of the church, waiting for my wife. The car was loaded with garbage for the dump, the remnants of last night's fish dinner making themselves known. Our border collie Tess was along on the mission. (I wished that I could have just sent her out to herd all the people to sign.) Mrs. Dennison came out of church first and showed me the letter of support she'd written to the paper. She loves writing, she told me. I looked it over quickly. "Pursuing" was spelled wrong. I didn't point this out; I thanked her. "Don't get a swelled head," she said. I replied by saying the suitably humble things required by this transaction.

Next came a blizzard of Congregationalists falling out of the church—Prescotts and Bemises and friendly folks that I chat with but whose names I can never remember.

I caught up with my wife in the minister's study. He looked much older. He had been through an ordeal. His flock had been roiling for months over whether to oust him. At a testy meeting about removing him, he had kept his job by the thinnest of margins, only six votes. But then the meeting voted to cut $21,000 in benefits, salary, and his housing allowance. They had just about pulled out his dental gold.

In his study he spoke bitterly of Hancock and his church as a false community. All the differences and anxieties are papered over, everyone makes nice. Then *blam!* there's an explosion of anger toward the leader because "needs" aren't being "met"; a chasm is revealed. An emptiness. A counterfeit community is uncovered, the daily currency of life has been shown to be worthless as sure as Confederate currency turned to litter in the hands of the bearer.

People feel cheated. They feel like they've been pressed into a one-dimensional picture. They are worn out, worn flat by pleasantries and chitchat and the polite formalities of this committee and that.

We all want to be liked by our neighbors. We all want to be nice, but it takes a toll. If people find themselves acting falsely, they feel corroded from within.

This is my translation. That morning the minister only spoke of false community and "needs" not being "met" and the group swallowing its leader alive. His anger left little room in his study for visitors.

I knew the minister pretty well. Over long dinners, we had listened to him preach against the town. His opposition was obvious. His desk did not face out to the common and Main Street, but inward toward two large photos he'd taken of the ranch he and his family retreated to in Wyoming. He took it personally that a large part of his flock came to church only because it was a community activity. They weren't on a spiritual journey. They weren't wrestling with questions of faith but with whose turn it was to make the coffeecake for the gathering afterwards.

In his sermons he thundered at those who showed up for showing up. I thought that this was a bad approach and told him so. He used to rehearse the major points of his sermons on me when I ran into him as I was picking up our mail in town. I suggested a less confrontational tack: at least they were in the pews every Sunday; perhaps he could ease them toward a religious journey. But he never relented. He had a "death wish," one friend told me, and indeed he soon parted from the congregation.

After that uplifting visit, we had to be going; people were waiting for us. We raced up Norway Hill to visit one of the library trustees. We sat for tea—I had coffee since it was expedient—and chatted with the trustee, her husband, and their daughter and son-in-law. The trustee jumped up to get the signature of an older conservative woman who was bedridden with pneumonia! I wisely declined to visit and sent her. We entertained her daughter and son-in-law with the details of this momentous election. They did find all this tumult amusing, a tempest in an empty teapot.

We hopped up and dashed off to get two more signatures from friends who should have been returning from making their Sunday visit to a legally blind old woman. We looked for them along the road, but couldn't find them, so we sprinted off to call on an acquaintance, Shelley, who had lived in town for thirty years.

Shelley told us about Hancock driving off its ministers over the years and speculated that it was because of all the retired folk who have nothing better to do. I'd heard this from a friend about the library: some people feel that all the big things of the world are out of control, but they could control this little library.

Shelley also told us about the novels she had just read

by the Egyptian Nobel Prize winner, Naguib Mahfouz. He takes this ordinary family life, she said, and he just opens it up and shows it to you. Everyone in the State Department should read it, she said. We may think that deep down everyone is the same. Wrong.

Her back room was full of sunlight and greenery, as were all the rooms I had visited. It was a flat-roofed modern room appended to an early 1800s Cape, all glass and views to a rolling pasture. Most of our houses have the solace of a view, of trees and fields and water, or of a few other handsome old houses nearby. Whether this lulls one to sleep or gives one a quiet, still center from which to engage the world depends on the person. They may be hiding from themselves and the world. They may have moved to "the country" to retreat or, instead, to "drive life into a corner" and "know it by experience," as Thoreau wrote in *Walden*. It's easy enough to lose a useful anger, a proper awareness of all those who wake up hungry every day. There is the danger of a strong *I've-got-mine* satisfaction. That's been the city mouse brief against country life since Virgil.

We hurried out and drove back to the village where we picked up our two friends who had been visiting the legally blind woman. Tess was barking wildly. The old fish remains in the garbage were starting to stink up the car. I dropped off our friends, stopped at the dump, and returned home to drop off my wife and Tess. I called two folks and drove back into the village.

At the home of a woman who has led many town committees, we discussed her cats, the view, and the trustee race. I brought up all the other topics, glad not to discuss the race. It was a pleasure to be in a house that I passed all the time. It had seemed to be sitting too close to the road. But inside the house opens up and embraces views of a private wooded preserve.

I am endlessly fascinated with the way people inhabit old houses—what they make new, what they leave alone; how they ennoble, change, or degrade a place.

Her house had an updated kitchen with a sweep of vinyl flooring that stopped like a sea at the edge of two-hundred-year-old floorboards. We make accommodations with the past. Big hand-hewn beams and a wall of picture-window glass. It works. 1820 and 1950 and 2000. Things accumulate, change, time moves on. I find these old/new/old houses much more interesting than fussy reproductions, or "period" houses suffocating on a diet of only antiques.

From there I stopped at Katherine's—again a sunny room—and nearby at another friend's house, before I called on the legally blind woman who, living on Main Street, was like the hub of a slowly wheeling galaxy. She doesn't go out much, but a steady procession of friends and neighbors stops by daily. She has a cozy of suite rooms in the Sheldon House, built in 1787—the oldest house in the village, she said.

The Sheldon House had a worn, shambling feeling. She showed me a big board—one that she said was illegal to have before the Revolution—and the crooked floors and her collection of giraffe figures. Many years ago she had lived in Africa.

She took out a big magnifying glass, studied the letter, leaning close like Sherlock Holmes looking for evidence, and signed it.

One more visit remained, with Alice, out on a dirt road near the town line. We sat for a while and talked about her reporting for the local paper and how difficult it is if she offends someone by taking a stand. She didn't want to make trouble for herself. She was weighing whether to sign my letter. In small towns you are granted just a small amount of political capital, so you have to choose your spots carefully. A disagreement can cast a long shadow, lingering for decades. But if you silence yourself, deferring to your neighbors, you can end up quarrelling with yourself for years, running through the same arguments over and over as if you were caught on one of those hamster exercise wheels.

We got to talking about the old Brown Insurance building in nearby Peterborough. She was surprised that I knew about that. Her father used to run the place and she worked there during the summer. Then she smiled. Not broadly, but a smile edging out, an easing that softened her. I know that she has suffered. One of her sons had killed himself; a loss that never leaves her. I've seen her stopping at her son's grave.

Just that day, as I was cleaning up the newspapers, I came across her weekly column. "Life's not fair," she had written. "It's not supposed to be." She used an example of two little kids fighting over who's going to do the chores, but I read it as a story about the loss of her son. We get from stories what we bring to them, and in small towns, we may bring entire lives to the reading, and sometimes a simple story runs deep.

At last I was home. I had seen some of Hancock at home on a snowy Sunday in February. All of us living here as if we'd always lived here and always would. All of us pretending this is just a comfortable old world we live in, as cozy as a nicely worn sweater.

Pain and suffering, disappointment and hopes and dreams—all are out of sight on the last day of February, but all are as present as the granite sleeping under the snow, and the mice in the walls awaiting their midnight rounds.

THE PEOPLE IN THE PHOTO

I. A FUNERAL

We file into the meetinghouse for a funeral. This takes some time. The meetinghouse, built in 1820, slows us to a ceremonial, processional pace. You don't enter this old house of worship, music, and government as you would enter a modern building, in one level approach with only the parting of automatic doors to mark the passage from the outside.

There's a lobby and a room with a stage—a complete, but petite theatrical stage—where the town has governed itself since the nineteenth century. This is the home of annual and special town meetings.

The church is upstairs. In my town church and state are separate but close neighbors. The meetinghouse is owned jointly by the church and the town. Both share the cost of the building's upkeep. It's one of the few in New Hampshire still like this.

Two tightly spiraling stairs lead to the sanctuary. The stairs land in an anteroom, which seems to have no use except to slow down the seating of the church. You always run into friends and neighbors who have come up the other stairs, or who have pooled there in cocktail-party clusters of conversation. This room houses the natural reluctance most people have to enter a church; it's a last of secular air.

The stairs to the balcony lead from this room. I often sit up there. The balcony is steeply pitched and you hover over the rest of the gathering. Looking down on your neighbors in their pews, the church is revealed as a ship on a voyage. All of us sitting quietly as we wait for the family to enter, the church organ thrumming like a ship's motor in the hull, a deep heart beating. This is why I sit up there, to remind myself that whatever the reason we are gathered—wedding or funeral, a Bach partita or the matter of taxes—we are all in this together, on the same voyage, whether we like it or not.

Today, the funeral is for a woman who died unexpectedly at age eighty-five in a car accident. She knew most everyone in town, volunteered all over, and was a big part of Old Home Day. We are prone to dismissing anyone in their eighties as having lived long enough, but she was vibrant and active; her death was premature. Her brother in Texas is one hundred years old and judging from his letter, which is read aloud, still sharp.

In the church we have sorted ourselves by age; only the younger folks have elected to take the extra flight of stairs to the balcony. We look down on gray heads, white heads, bald heads. We look down on most of the people who define the town for me, who are the town. Their past leadership, their humor and grace, has made this a good place to live. I am struck with a horrible thought: We're going to have to go to all their funerals. That's the next voyage. I miss them already.

The woman's children and grandchildren rise and testify to her love for them. "She always told me: I love you. Remember you're special." They speak of happy times at the beach, of her friendly but determined competitive streak in tennis or Scrabble, and of letters, phone calls, and visits, always ending with: "Remember, I love you."

It's a perfect memorial and it almost capsizes the ship. The funeral upsets the elders downstairs. Not only have they lost a friend but they are thinking: *My children, my grandchildren will never speak this well about me. Will they even show up? My funeral won't be this good. I'm not as good a grandmother as she was. My grandchildren aren't as good as hers. My family isn't as close as hers. My funeral will never equal this.*

The stock market of emotions never closes. We keep measuring ourselves against others. This also happens at weddings and bar mitzvahs when we see accomplished children and super-wonderful families. Happy families can be oppressive.

Wrath and love may walk hand-in-hand at Town Meeting, as Ralph Waldo Emerson said, but envy and regret may stalk funerals and weddings. Pride and sorrow, the beginning of life and the end, we meet all this in the meetinghouse.

II. A FEW DEATHS AT DINNER

When I dine with older friends in their seventies and eighties, I have this dinner conversation in several variations. We drink wine and trade news about friends and local politics, but the talk slides toward illness, infirmity, and last things.

On this evening I join Rebecca and George for dinner in their new porch room. Rebecca had it painted a perfect light green. The proportions and the view are calming. I look at Rebecca and George, so comfortable in this life, and I want them to live forever. And again I feel the ashen horror of having to attend their funerals. I'd really much rather that they attend mine.

These thoughts are accompanied by Rebecca telling us about her Aunt Isabelle, who at age seventy-five got a brain tumor. She's been healthy her whole life and fit, never smoked, etc. She's in the hospital. Rebecca is shaken by this and visits her often. She has known Isabelle her whole life.

The other dinner guest is in his early sixties. He recounts his mother-in-law's brush with death, her "lucky aneurysm" as it has become known in the family.

She was stricken just as they were driving out of the Ted Williams Tunnel. They stopped. There was a cop across the way. They flagged him down. He raced them to Massachusetts General. Minutes later she was being operated on by the leading aneurysm expert in the country—he just happened to have finished an operation and they caught him before he left the hospital. He got to the aneurysm just before it would have ruptured. Even so, she had a long recovery and spoke gibberish for weeks. She's recovered now. The entire story turns on the word "just"—just in time, a lucky instant between life and death.

But poor Aunt Isabelle left the hospital and had to return twice, each a rough journey, once a six-hour ambulance ride in a snowstorm, and once by helicopter. She reaches for words and doesn't know them. She's weak on one side.

We live in a perilous amusement park. We ride up and down these roller coasters and Ferris wheels: marriage, kids, troubles, dinner parties, holidays, summer, winter, and summer again. And along the way, disease and death. It's the mix of forever and ever, the daily beat, on and on, and sudden death that's cruel. That tick-tock daily reassurance—all is ok, all is well, and *wham!* You're sick, you're dead, you are no more.

The lucky story leads to our hosts telling us an unlucky story, one thirty years old, a story that has understandably stayed with them. It's every parent's fear: A mother turns her back on her four-year-old to look after her infant, just

73

for a moment. He vanishes. In the same instant, a passing driver happens to see a little boy floating in the pond behind their house. This was lucky; it was a lonely country road. But the rest is sorrow: he pulls the little boy from the water, races to the hospital . . . too late. And all this in an instant, a few breaths of life's thousands.

One dinner and three tales of death and near death and coming death. The evening's score was mixed—death winning once, cheated once, and held to a draw, for now.

III. CHEMO

Annie enters the small café on Main Street to spontaneous cheers. It sounds like a wild ovation. Annie brightens. This homage is a gift. She's got cancer; she begins chemo this week. My wife tells her that Bonnie has lined up a battalion of ladies to cook her meals. "You are so loved," my wife tells her.

Annie says that at least she's lost weight. We make the usual jokes about this being a severe diet. She is much thinner, and the longer you take this in, the more worrying it is. She lingers by our table a little too long. We have a few more exchanges. She's really buoyed by this, but we've arrived at that awkward feeling when someone is towering over your table. We are with friends who don't know Annie and we feel them withdrawing, waiting this out. At the mention of the "C word" they curl into an armored ball. They have had a long, torturous run-in with the C word. For years they had to live in Cancer Country. They never want to return.

Still she lingers like a dinner guest missing the cues that the evening is over. She needs more of our assurance, our concern, before she's left alone again in Cancer Country, in the valley between life and death that is chemo. We offer some more encouragement and volunteer to help, before we excuse ourselves to ease the pain of our separateness, I suppose, and to ease our friends' growing darkness. One more thing we do for others.

IV. THE PEOPLE IN THE PHOTO

The people in the photo look out at us square on. They stand at attention. They stand as if they are as solid as rocks and just as eternal.

The people in the photo have no names. They had names and voices once, and complaints and aches and praise and fears, once. They were someone's son, someone's husband, someone's father, once. But all that has fallen away. We are left with objects in the landscape—a person, a house, a tree, the ground.

I have looked at a lot of old photos and what is interesting is often what is in the background—the style of a hat, the shape of a car fender, eyeglasses, the price of a loaf of bread. The people who are in that old picture live on not as themselves, with their humor and sorrows, but they live on as history, as an example of a typical haircut or a popular jacket.

This is also true of famous photos, the emblematic instants that we think we understand. The boy running from the factory in Lewis Hine's 1909 photo of the Manchester textile mills is now and for all times "child labor." Hine didn't get his name. The people on the steamer's lower deck in Alfred Stieglitz's 1907 photo of "The Steerage" are no longer their fears and hopes, but they are "immigration." (Even though the ship is actually *leaving* New York for Germany.) The lined, worried face of the "Migrant Mother" with an infant on her lap and two children hiding next to her in Dorothea Lange's Depression-era photo is "hard times." They live on as examples. Those outside the frame are statistics—rows of numbers like headstones in a cemetery.

These people, oh so old, oh so long gone.

We are the people in the photo. We may have posed eagerly in our Sunday best. We don't know what future ages will say about our era. We want them to admire our cleverness, to understand our failings, to overlook our cruelty. But time will reduce us to an example, to an instant, to a wink of our former selves, a detail of a moment. There we are in the unlabeled photos, someone's forgotten ancestor, someone's forgotten relative, another lucky instant in the universe.

A HOG'S LIFE

The first frost is a hog's holiday. It's as if the whole world tilts and vegetables roll toward the commodious jaws of our pig Christopher Hogwood: zucchinis the size of baseball bats, tomatoes that were caught on the vine, broccoli that has bolted, squash going soft in one spot.

Our friends, gardeners, come and render unto Hogwood that which is his. The dreams of the winter seed catalog, the toil of the blackfly season, the loyal watering of July, he takes it all in, joyfully grinds it down—grabs a pumpkin and shakes it from side to side, crushes a beet, snout upward, with red beet juice dripping from his jowls.

Everyone stands and watches. It is good theater. Our pig is a Zen eater. He becomes his food. He is his food. He loves his food. No remorse. No guilty dinner chat about fat or sugar or pesticides. A pig brings us back to a simpler time in our dining history. All food is good food.

Over the years Christopher Hogwood has built a larger constituency than most congressmen. He commands a slops empire that reaches from southern New Hampshire some 160 miles north to the shores of Lake Champlain. He receives weekly slops deliveries from Harlow Richardson's cheese shop in neighboring Peterborough. This has made him a discerning connoisseur of spoiled dill-Havarti cheese, sourdough bread, balsamic vinegar, red-leafed lettuce, and bagels—a dozen or more burned bagels in a bucket (until, tragically, Harlow got a new toaster). Our postmaster here in Hancock leaves him slops near the post office loading dock. The girls next door, Kate and Jane Cabot, have spoon-fed freezer-burned ice cream into his fearsome mouth (a mouth flanked by curving tusks). He cleans off the spoon and patiently stands with his lips set for the next helping. An international antelope specialist brings him slops. He has dined on the carcasses of a dozen lobster shells, a red claw or an antenna sticking out of his jaw, as in some monster movie, before he grinds the crustacean to a fine powder. And he has received a shipment of stale bread from a book editor up in Vermont (whose name we withhold to protect the employed).

This is only a partial list. For someone who spends most of his time in his pen or outside sunning himself, he can sure network. One time our new neighbors had made their first visit to church. After the service, as they shook hands with the minister on the church steps, he tried to place them. "Oh," he said, "you live near Christopher Hogwood."

He is in fact the most successful hog of his class—Class of '90, George and Mary Iselin's farm in Marlborough, New Hampshire—and quite likely the only pig of his class left alive. A pig's life is usually a six-month march from teat to trough to freezer. But young Mr. Hogwood was a runt, a sickly piglet that Mary called "the spotted thing."

They were going to have to hit him over the head with a shovel unless we'd take him. "He's a runt; he'll stay small," we were told. He arrived in a shoebox, all runny, and didn't utter a sound for weeks. We named him Christopher Hogwood after the artistic director of Boston's Handel & Haydn Society, an advocate of "early music." There is no earlier music than a hog's bellowing.

He got better and grew to the size of a cat—if a cat were built out of cast iron. He was fond of beer right out of the bottle. He was the right size for such behavior until I wormed him.

I swaggered into the local feed store, remembering my childhood years of watching *Modern Farmer* before the Saturday morning cartoons.

"I have to worm the swine herd," I announced.

"How many do you have?"

"One." I quickly covered with technical talk: "A one-shoat piggery." (Shoats, you'd know if you watched *Modern Farmer*, are young weaned pigs.)

We wormed him, and the rest, as they say, is lard. He has been on a steady growth curve for years. He weighs six hundred pounds. (Pig-o-metrics: length x girth x girth divided by 400 = weight.) He has been appraised as a lean bacon hog with eyes like the actor Claude Rains (who played the cynical police chief in *Casablanca*). He looks like an advertisement for volumetric space.

It's a hog's life—food, visitors, and media attention. After an appearance on a Boston TV show, he broke out of his pen. In the police log, Ed Coughlan, Hancock's police chief, said, "He can't take the publicity."

Another time, Ed caught up with him after he'd gotten out. Hogs are always watching you, studying locks and latches.

"Is this your pig?" he said, as Hogwood, then a sprightly three hundred pounds, pulled at the rope he had on him. Ed is given to understatement.

"Book him. Teach him a lesson. Take him to the meat aisle of the A&P. Throw a scare into him." That's what I wanted to say.

"Yeah," is all I said.

As people watch him grunting with pleasure or smashing peach pits with his teeth, they step back and ask:

"Will you eat him?"

"No."

"How long do pigs live?"

"No one really knows. Seven, thirteen, eighteen years. The stories have come in."

I asked the agricultural agent at the state fair about porcine longevity, and he was visibly annoyed by my question.

Ag. agents know that boutique piggeries are the death knell of agriculture. You have people coddling hogs and letting lambs live on to collect Social Security, and soon there are no farms and no ag. agents.

I have known many people who set out to be their own homestead butcher, but year by year the hogs wore them down. The hogs were intelligent, cunning, affectionate, each different from the next. They'd name them and would remember them years after they'd forgotten some friends. There was the one who followed them everywhere, the one who learned how to jump high over the fence. . . .

They'd reach a breaking point. They could no longer kill them. Pigs are too much like us. They love company. They love to sleep in the sun. And they're greedy—they have *needs*.

Watch a pig eat on enough mornings and you'll learn an essential truth: Appetite makes the world go 'round. Hunger for wealth, for power, for knowledge, for love. All the great mystics and financiers have realized that appetite sets the world spinning.

That's one big lesson to learn from one pig, but then that's one big pig.

PLANTING ELMS

Some people buy lottery tickets; we plant elms. We plant them hoping that these spindly saplings will dodge Dutch elm disease and outrun the other elm pathogens to rise up in their graceful vase form and maybe even become a "great, green cloud swelling in the horizon," as Oliver Wendell Holmes described one magnificent elm.

Holmes made pilgrimages to be in the presence of great trees, majestic elms bearing names like The Pride of the State, The Green Tree, The Divine Elm. They have an ethereal quality in old photos: solid at the trunk, but the crown is ghost-like, more light than leaf, like the kind of light that shines in biblical illustrations of heaven. A trick of the camera and the need for a long exposure. These great ones were the best of their generation. There were millions of elms. Every city had its Elm Street where the branches formed a cathedral nave of deep shade and stunning gold in the fall. "Nothing finer has been given us and nothing finer could be wished for," said one forestry college dean. Elms were the landscape of America.

Dutch elm disease took them all except for a few surprising survivors that have been studied and bred to try to create a disease-resistant elm. From the contenders we chose the Princeton elm, which some say has the best survival rate. We planted four in our pasture, naming them after the few Princetonians that we knew. F. Scott Fitzgerald and his friend the critic Edmund Wilson were the first two we planted. They came in the mail as little whippy sticks.

Elms are celebrated for their swift growth, but Fitzgerald and Wilson have been slow to catch. It didn't help that Fitzgerald was trampled by sheep who knocked him sideways and ate almost all of his few leaves. We righted him, and put cages around both trees. For years poor Fitzgerald looked like those photos of his namesake in his last alcohol-ravaged days, but he has slowly recovered. His friend Wilson is robust, a model elm, though diminutive—a mini-elm—still. We may have accidently developed the apartment-dweller's elm: Put out a dozen in pots on your terrace to create a petite *grande allée*. (Perhaps it would have been smarter to name one after basketball star Bill Bradley.)

We followed these two by planting trees too big to be trampled, six feet tall. Woodrow Wilson has been stubborn, steadily growing, as you might expect. Albert Einstein though has had some thinning in his crown. Each spring I think that this is the year that the trees will flourish. Meanwhile in the woods around the pasture, elms shoot up, reach that moment when they're about to shed their adolescent awkwardness, and then they die. I suppose I should just cut them down as they appear, but if someone gave you a lottery ticket, would you just throw it out? One of these young elms could be a great-tree-in-waiting, the next Divine Elm.

Our quartet of starter trees would disappoint Holmes, I'm sure. We share his veneration for *Ulmus americana*, and also his selective sight. Elms are grand, but they are also symbolic of how we want to rearrange the world, cultivating some plants as flowers and damning others as weeds, revering some animals and exterminating others. Biologists call the big, attention-getting creatures we love "charismatic megafauna": the pandas, elephants, and tigers that draw the crowds in zoos, the endangered eagles, loons, and bears that grace the fundraising newsletters of environmental groups.

This is our weakness. The "poster child" species may win attention for an entire ecosystem, but this is also a species of blindness. Millions are spent to restore salmon to their upstream migration while the less-photogenic shortnose sturgeon is left to swim for itself. We pick and choose. We cultivate food, flowers, and shade trees, but we also cultivate loss. We are the poorer for this approach. It was the love of elms that doomed them. Just planting one type of anything is a bad practice. But whenever I come across an old surviving elm, I, too, am an instant convert. I'd plant elms by the millions.

DRIVING BLIND

Some years ago an elderly woman hereabouts hit a flag-man. I'll repeat that: While driving on a clear, sunny day, she ran into a six-foot-tall man who was wearing a Day-Glo orange vest and holding a big Stop sign. She didn't see him. She was well past eighty then with a mole-like squint and, as was admitted afterwards, legally blind. She'd been living in a shadowland for years. She lost her license. The flagman was shaken, but not broken.

We can only imagine what the state highway workers said, but for years after this, they were very jumpy when working on our lightly traveled country roads. We were marked on the maps: *Here be (blind) dragons.*

That's the story as it was told around town. This report was followed by a roster of Driving Blind stories. Do you remember, someone would say, when Kathy went over the edge of the post office parking lot? No one was harmed. She just plunged a short ways down the green hill to the pond.

When Ed, our unflappable police chief, arrived, he looked at her car as it was being winched back uphill. "Kathy, what's this stripe on the side of your car?" he asked. "Oh that? That's Colin. He hit me there last week," she said. Colin was another blind driver. When she went to get back into her car Ed insisted, gently, that perhaps it would be best if he drove her home. "It's like bumper cars out there," he later told us.

Other stories followed, usually about women because they tend to outlive the men. Do you remember the woman who lived up the hill driving down Main Street? She wore those big, wraparound cataract sunglasses—oversized visors. And when she got out of her car she'd feel for the handle of the door to the post office. And do you remember Amanda mistaking the accelerator for the brake and launching her car backwards through the window of the pharmacy? No one was hurt. Her little dogs in the back seat, however, were a little rattled. "I don't think they'll be riding back there anymore," said the cop on the scene.

At one time we had so many ancient drivers—drivers of questionable vision—that I proposed we put up a board in the center of town to track them—little flashing lights would tell you where they were on our local roads. We could pause, survey the blinking lights, and choose a safe route. It would make a good Eagle Scout project.

Yes, we were having a laugh on the old timers. They are funny stories—they're tragicomic. People *could* be killed, but they're not. We're mocking growing older. It's like little kids who run up and ring the bell on the scary house in the neighborhood. These are campfire horror stories. But there's more to it than that. We tell these stories out of fear and admiration. We fear that this will happen to us; we admire them for resisting. We fear meeting them on the road; we admire a society that still has space for this sort of eccentric and, yes, dangerous behavior. We haven't sanded down all the rough spots—yet.

To lose your license is to lose your citizenship. You have to rely on others for favors—if you're lucky. If you're unlucky you're invisible, shut in with your aging self. It's a return to an enfeebled childhood. So who can summon the common sense to tell them not to drive blind? They have been worn by winter after New England winter, by war and career, marriage and children. They've seen it all in their lives. They know where the roads go; they know the outline by heart. More looking would just be folly.

But then at one dinner, after we'd fallen into these stories, a friend of ours upped the ante. She told us that Betsey had set out for her house and never showed up. Betsey called saying that she'd driven around for a long time but couldn't remember where our friend lived. Betsey has lived here her entire life.

We all sagged. Another friend said that, on the other hand, the other morning Betsey said that she'd bring something over and she went home and came back and she'd done it.

Yes, someone else said, it's not a straight decline, and he made a motion with his hand that indicated a downward trend marked by plateaus.

We sat quietly for a moment. No one wanted to follow the plunging line with similar stories. The formula for the Driving Blind stories couldn't carry us into this new territory.

All the stories of Driving Blind are about whistling past the graveyard, about exulted individuals standing against fate and death. We want to believe that the self will prevail against the encroaching darkness. If it means being the village eccentric, well then fine. Better that than sitting in a nursing home wheelchair looking like a deflated toy balloon.

We love survivor's tales. We flock to the men and women who walked out of the death camps to write uplifting memoirs, to be a witness against injustice. We want the tales of the Boat People who scrimp for their children to go through the Ivy League and become Big Deal American Dreams. We want young entrepreneurs who sketch out their invention on a restaurant napkin and build it in a garage and within a few years live in a perpetual ticker-tape parade of adulation. (These stories always start with napkins and garages.) We want the mountain climber who, after losing both legs to frostbite on a bad winter hike, rises up to invent new prosthetic limbs, returns to climbing, and gives a rousing TED talk about the triumph of the human spirit. We want our flame to burn as pure in the face of the climb that is forced on all of us as we age.

That's what these tales of Driving Blind are about—conquering aging, saying stupid things like sixty is the new forty, or dementia is the new—*what?* We want to say, look at so and so; eighty-five and just back from France and she drank us under the table past midnight. If that's eighty-five, bring it on. (Yes, that's eighty-five, but for her, not necessarily for you.)

We don't want the body to have its say—which is always final, always a veto. We want to vote with our cherished personalities. We want aging on our own terms; we want to die in our sleep. But we don't get to choose. Genetics, fate, mortality, biology—the oldest Greek chorus—have their say.

The roster of Driving Blind stories are told in homage, out of a slightly crizzled respect. All honor is due those who are independent to the very last, who drive over a cliff like some blind and aging Thelma and Louise—even if by accident, in reverse.

MENDING FENCES

I have been fixing the same old pasture fence for more than twenty years and in that time the fence has educated me. This old horse fence, unpainted wooden boards and posts, has schooled me in wood and tools.

George Iselin built this fence seventeen years before we bought our house with its old barn, outbuilding, and eight acres of fields and woods along the Moose Brook. George is as deceptive as his fence. He looks like an unkempt, wispy hippie. In his college years he was known on campus for going barefoot in the New Hampshire winter. But George is incredibly strong (and kind). He works as a farrier, and I have seen him move a heavy heating oil tank by himself that would have normally taken two or more people to move. His fence is strong like him: he nailed it together with huge spikes. All of the fence posts are standing tough—no rot, not the least little wiggle in any of them after nearly forty years. Most of his thick boards are still hanging there; some of my replacement boards have come and gone while his lichen-covered boards hang there. Why? This fence should have fallen apart long ago.

At first I was slow to realize my caretaking duties. Our pasture is right on a major road to town, so I knew that I had to keep the fence up, but I was always behind and unprepared. For starters, I had no power tools. To replace a board, I had to pry out those huge rusty nails—they were as long as railroad spikes. Sometimes I had to throw all my weight behind the pry bar. Then I'd cut a new board with my old hand saw. It was slow going.

It was worse keeping the fence line clear. Brush had grown right under the fence. I went at the fence line with some dangerous tools, including a rented brush cutter that had a naked circular saw blade dancing and hopping at the end of a long handle. Then I graduated to a chainsaw, which wasn't much better. I'd do this every few years in the summer, and haul pickup truckloads to the burn pile at the dump. But it seemed that every time I looked across the field at the fence, all the brush had sprung back, as if seen in some time-lapse movie.

I could have let the fence fall down, coming apart season after season, until it looked like a child's game of pick-up sticks. But that would be letting down the team. I kept up the fence for my neighbors, not so they'll think better of me, but so they'll feel that all is right with the world. We tend to take outward appearances as inward reports: upright fence, upright life. Trim house, trim life.

We are surprised when, time and again, the opposite is true. We know the scene well: The news van broadcasting in front of the beautiful house that is the site of the ugly crime. The neighbors looking into the cameras to say that they had no idea—*he was such a nice man.* The news cameras scanning the front of the well-tended house looking for signs of guilt. The entire town may be put into a kind of police lineup: the fine churches and parks all serving to ask: *How could this happen here?*

Even if an upright fence is not a picture postcard of a happy universe, it's better than being sloppy. So I finally wised up and called in a backhoe to uproot the brush. I got a new fleet of cordless tools—a small circular saw to cut the boards, and a reciprocating saw to cut the old nails off.

George's fence taught me all this. If you drive by and see a guy fixing a fence, you'd have it wrong. It's really a fence getting a guy to keep it standing. This is what Michael Pollan says plants do: we are working to spread apples or potatoes. The plants are cleverly in charge.

But lately the fence has been showing its age. (I don't know about George.) We had a few snowy winters and the plows pushed the snow hard against the fence. In spring it looked like a stampede had busted through the boards. I have had the dreaded end-of-life discussions with my wife: *Should we just take it down?*

At first we fixed the fence to keep horses in, but sheep

are pastured there now and they have their own portable fencing. So we fixed the fence for appearance sake. And now we fix it because it would be just too much work to take it down. (The posts still stand true.) It's easier to leave it. I try not to think about this as I fix the fence each year, try not to see it as metaphor for life or the politics of our republic. I just patch the fence. It's what the fence wants.

SUMMER OVER AUTUMN

Floating, paddle at rest, my kayak is adrift in the middle of the pond as I look at the mountain. It's mid-August. The light is silvery and soft. I can see a weakening of the green, and here and there like a splattering of paint, the first yellow leaves.

Autumn is beginning to slip out from undercover. I think of this moment as its own distinct time, as "Summer Over Autumn." This is the moment that precedes the fall snap, the great colors, and the final bare season in November.

Summer is in high season—you'll never eat better tomatoes or corn, but the first apples are ready for picking, the evenings are cooler, and the day's heat lacks conviction. Summer at this moment is a party, but the party is already over. August in northern New England is poignant, a quick curtain call for the green earth, for summer's heat, and for the gardens.

Summer Over Autumn isn't a season. It's a glimpse, the moment when we see the skull beneath the skin, the death that is always part of life. "In the midst of life we are in death," as the *Book of Common Prayer* says.

It's a moment poised on the seesaw, right at the fulcrum, a moment of passage. Sitting still, you can feel summer passing, retreating as fog retreats. It's like passing through a doorway. If we could inhabit a still-point, floating as if we were in a kayak, would we be aware of the many doorways we daily pass through?

The pond is one such doorway. We have seen loons nest, raise a fluffy, awkward chick, and then at season's end, fly off. None of this looks easy, and each summer it seems as if the loons are inventing it all over again—the way the chick at first rides on the mother's back, then the stage where it is on its own in the water, but looks like a floating toupee. And when the loons are getting ready to fly away, they have to flap their way down the length of the pond to rise just a few feet. To clear the trees, they have to circle again. They look less like birds than someone earnestly impersonating a bird.

Turtles; snakes; salamanders; the occasional otter family; a bald eagle fishing; pink lady's slipper orchids; dragonflies; kingfishers; big rocks that have shifted, fissured, and shed parts of themselves; tall trees that shaded us one summer, died the next, and by and by fell over, giving rise to other trees, plants, and insects. All these we have seen at this one pond while adrift.

And we have seen people come and go. There was a young couple who lived in a small cottage near the pond. I'd see them working on their place. None of that came easy, either. He always seemed to have a circular saw in one hand; she was balancing a baby on her hip, and keeping her eye on their two-year-old, while trying to hold a board for him. She looked as tired as those women in the photos from the Depression-era Dust Bowl.

For a couple of summers, I'd walk past them in this formation, or stop sometimes to chat. What happened next happened in winter, I guess. They separated and divorced. He got very sick, and I last saw him in town. He was confused, under heavy medication, and too thin, the death in him showing. He died not long after; other couples have come to live out their dramas in that cottage.

Summer Over Autumn will never make the roster of mini seasons like Mud Season and Black Fly Season. It's just too short. It's like a ferry ride described long ago by the eighth-century Chinese poet, Tu Fu: a group of "dandies" and young women set out on a fine summer's day but, as Carolyn Kizer translates:

Above us a patch of cloud spreads, darkening
Like a water-stain on silk.

The women in their "crimson skirts" are drenched by a downpour. The ferry trip home is cold and wet.

Like a knife in a melon, Autumn slices Summer.

THE UNITED STATES OF RUIN

I. LEAVING

The business of America is leaving. In Iowa, a 1930 list of abandoned towns, villages, and post offices counted 2,205 lost places in nearly one hundred years. A survey in Kansas found more than 2,500 "extinct geographical locations." An 1893 history of a small town in Massachusetts recorded 101 "abandoned homesteads," a geography of the missing. "A striking feature of the territory of town at the present day . . . is the appearance, here and there in all directions, of old cellars, wells, orchards, or other tokens of dwellings once existing but now gone forever," the town history reports. Many of the descendants of founding families—Brooks, Graves, Heywood, Hoar, Taylor—had gone west. Jamestown, Virginia, it can be argued, set the pace: established in 1607 as the first permanent English settlement, it served as state capital until 1698, but by 1722 there were only three or four inhabited houses amid an "abundance of Brick Rubbish." Geographers call this the "pattern of settlement and abandonment."

The way west was littered with the ruins of the old homestead, with trunks and chairs, keepsakes and graves. What had seemed important at the journey's start was thrown over as if they were throwing over their old lives back east. Heading west, James Abbey, who left Indiana for California in 1849, wrote in his diary about crossing the desert as he approached the Sierra Nevadas: "I counted in a distance of fifteen miles 350 dead horses, 280 oxen, and 120 mules. . . . Vast amounts of valuable property have been abandoned and thrown away in this desert—leather trunks, clothing, wagons, etc." Lighten up the load and light out for the territory. Keep moving.

That's still our M. O. (The way to the moon was strewn with trash as stage after stage of the rocket fell away to become space junk.) Don't look back. Settle and sell, mine and move. Walk out on your mortgage if you must, declare bankruptcy, and start all over. It's a tradition. Care for an abandoned house? A few square miles of empty factories or mills? A mall? (Twenty percent of all malls are troubled by high vacancy rates or they are dying.) How about a skyscraper or even a downtown—Detroit? Make an offer. Detroit's 90,000 empty lots may outnumber its buildings.

"The lesson is this: when migration turns to a new region, do not clutch the dying past. Let go and move on," advises real estate economist Jack Lessinger. "Steadfast in its consensus, the economy becomes a veritable bulldozer programmed to scrape out, heap up, and reshape the world to its own special images." You can either feed the scrapheap or be on it. Seize the day and leave.

Our national anthem is *jump!* Or it could be what Philip Hone wrote: *"Overturn! Overturn! Overturn!"* That is "the maxim of New York," the former mayor wrote in 1845. "The very bones of our ancestors are not permitted to lie quiet a quarter of a century, and one generation of men seem studious to remove all the relics of those which preceded them." (Hone was not only speaking metaphorically. The young Walt Whitman took up the cause of a woman defending the graves of her husband and family from the land speculators who had arrived to dig it up. A mob joined her and rioted.)

Welcome to the United States of Ruin, land of abandonment. We'll abandon anything and move on. We have an ever-growing lexicon of waste and ruin: hazardous waste sites, "brownfields," ammo dumps, open-pit mines, "national sacrifice areas," fences around weedy lots that no one dare survey, or as some planners class them: LOOs, LULUs, NIMBYs, and TOADs (Waste Landscapes of Obsolescence, Locally Unwanted Land Use, Not in My Backyard, and Temporary, Obsolete, Abandoned, or Derelict sites).

Traveling the country you will find abandoned houses, churches, mills, bridges, grain elevators, storefronts, orphaned thirty-story-tall chimneys from smelters, and empty Air Force plutonium storage vaults. You'll pass houses arrested in flight, caught in the act of moving—the house jacked up on wooden rails, waiting to leave. Did someone move it here? Or were they going to move it and just gave up? Moving houses is an American tradition.

A history of ruins is a history of roads. Our houses are often on the move. Ruins are just one stop—one frame—in this time-lapse of coming and going. We are the ghosts in this landscape—the image moving too fast—blurring—in the photograph.

A local historian was looking at a nineteenth century map of a small town in northern New Hampshire. He had been digging into his family history and had thus far not come up with any great founders or great scoundrels. "This is where my people came to," he said, touching a few names on the map, family names next to the black squares representing houses. "They didn't do so well," he said. Those houses are cellar holes today and his people are a long time gone from that town. Cellar holes and ruins are the history written by the rest of us. We show up, muddle along or fail, and move on. We don't make it into the town history; we don't leave our names on schools and monuments and roads.

We are all camping out here, in houses of wood and brick, in office buildings of cement and steel. Tents in the wilderness. It's all temporary. If we clear a field, the woods will have it back soon enough. If we dam a river, it bides its time and will resume its true course. The land forgets us even as we are here. We light our fires, brighten our homes, and delight in our conquest. But we're not even a thought in the mind of this land. The land dreams granite and maple and pine, deer and wolf and beaver. We white settlers are but a momentary incursion. And all our lives are like water over granite.

II. GAINING

We tell ourselves two stories about home. One is Rip Van Winkle's story. He falls asleep in the hills for twenty years and awakens to find his hometown changed beyond recognition. We know in our bones that Rip Van Winkle is a story with some truth. New lives press in behind us and won't be denied. All that we hold and love falls from our grasp. Home leaves us.

The other story we tell ourselves is the traveler's tale. Out on the road, out at sea (as so many songs have it), gone for years and years, we can return. The lamp is in the window, the fire is on the hearth. Home waits for us.

The abandoned house contains both stories of home. We enter to find that home has left. We enter to see what remains. Can we rekindle the hearth?

What we find in ruins is a kind of melancholy. Free of

clutter, free of us, a house gains stillness. It is a kind of stillness that we find on old country roads. It's the skeleton, the death inside us. It's the clock ticking our days away. We lack a good word for this kind of going away, this decay in which something else is present. Ghost or ruin doesn't convey it. The Japanese call this feeling *mono no aware*, defined as the bittersweet sadness of things as they are, or a sensitivity to the fleeting beauty of the world. "You accept it, you even in a small way celebrate it, this evanescence," says Donald Richie, a lifelong student of Japanese culture. "You are to observe what is happening, and be content that things are proceeding as they must, and therefore should."

In the land of The Next Big Thing, ruins are like preserves of *mono no aware*. A ruin invites us to enter; it is ours alone to inhabit. We can be the ghost of the future come to visit, to render a judgment if we care. Prowling an abandoned house we can spy on ourselves and imagine what our house will be like when we are gone. It's like placing a call to a phone in an empty apartment. Though we know better, we can't help but imagine that we are hearing the phone itself ring in that empty room.

The ruin provides a setting we recognize—the outlines of home—but it has softened. In the outline we see not the house and hearth so much, but time and quiet. We see that we are here and gone. We see, as best we are able, time itself. Time shifts and the ruin may seem not as if it is going away, but as if it is coming toward us, gaining on us, insisting on our own mortality.

III. WHAT REMAINS

From time to time I visit a farmhouse and barn that is packed with old furniture for sale. Each room is thick with oak dining tables, ponderous Second Empire break-fronts, massive desks, the once-grand and the once-modest. But I am drawn to the attic. It is stuffed with chairs. The chairs stand obediently in rows, fading away into the dark recesses of the sloping attic walls. Many of them are still in their family groups of two, four, or even six. Each tagged, each an immigrant, they stand together as if they had been plucked in mid-sentence from their old kitchens and dining rooms.

How many chairs? Three hundred, four hundred? How many breakfasts and Sunday dinners, meals over good news and bad, meals eaten in a sullen silence? Some of those chairs have enough character to cast a play. The taut-ness of their attention makes it seem as if they are watching you, awaiting your verdict.

Like any waiting room, it's a mongrel democracy. Striving high-style chairs are pressed up against plain, poor chairs—chairs that were the cheapest of their day, now as worn as old overalls. Here are the once-sunny yellows, the dark-beyond-dark formal dining chairs, the round shoulders of simple Windsors, smudgy reds, faded apple-greens, broken bottoms, and chairs halfway to refinishing, traces of paint remaining, looking as if they had weathered a sandstorm only to be left in limbo, a kind of double abandonment.

The attic has wide boards, each two feet across, and the remains of one small finished room, which would have been off by itself, it seems, away from the main house. The room has grand wallpaper with a wide floral border scaled for a formal Victorian parlor. (Was this wallpaper to compensate for the guilt of isolating a family member back here? Someone sick or insane? Or was this a maid's room?) Today the paper is peeling and billowing, giving the sloping walls a tent-like feeling. There's one narrow dormer window with a gauzy white curtain, and the light pulls you toward it to look out, freed for a moment from the chairs.

In the last few years, some memorials have been built with empty chairs—as at Oklahoma City to commemorate the bombing of the federal building—but they lack the concentrated insistence of these chairs. There are chairs here that started out with newlyweds that may have seen an entire life's journey from firstborn to grandchildren, from last illness to death. Some of these chairs were cast out for something new, but most of them were likely from the end of life, when a son or daughter or neighbors or strangers had to "break up the house."

The attic is a dense and moving memorial to ordinary time, to breakfast-lunch-and-dinner, over and over, again and again. Lined up like stones in a cemetery, the chairs are witnesses that seem to be on the edge of speech. They are empty, but still carrying the weight of all the lives that had sat there. They have that quality we see in abandoned houses—call it an emptiness that is full, or the presence of an implied life. Someone has just left the room.

THE CLOCKWINDER

One summer day in 1965, Bob Fogg was at the Hancock town dump when one of the selectmen said to him: "Hey, Bob, you've got a lot of free time, how'd you like to take care of the town clock?" "And I didn't know anything about it," says Bob, "but I did know that the clock was stopped at ten minutes of six. It wasn't working."

Fogg examined the clock with another selectman and found that a pin had come loose, jamming the gears. They hammered in a new pin, and then they found a packet of old papers that helped them figure out how to run the 1872 tower clock in the meetinghouse. The strike—the gears that cause the hammer to hit the big bell—has to be wound one crank for each hour. It's a heavy crank that pulls about five hundred pounds of weight in a chute that runs sixty-five feet to the meetinghouse basement. The much lighter time train, which keeps the clock ticking, has to be wound seventy turns a week.

He was twenty-seven years old that summer, and he thought nothing of racing up the steep steps and throwing his weight against the heavy crank that sets the striker. He'd turn a week's worth—168 cranks—without a pause. On hot days, temperature in the nineties, he'd leave behind a pool of sweat. Now he's seventy-three, though you wouldn't know it. He's trim and his face is unlined. He takes his time coming up the stairs, rests before cranking, and he breaks the week's winding up into two or three visits. Even though twenty cranks will leave him winded, he's fit. He works out at the local gym every weekday at 5:30 a.m.

"I can't even remember back when I was twenty-seven, it was so long ago. I was a kid then. I could run up the stairs and crank away those weights and run back down and not even be breathing hard," he says.

Fogg knew nothing about clocks. He hadn't even known that anyone had to wind the town clock. He had grown up spending summers in town, served in the navy, and worked in one of the town garages. So he took some adult education courses about clocks at the middle school. They took apart clocks, cleaned, adjusted, and reassembled them. The tower clock, made by E. Howard & Co. in Boston, has the same parts as other clocks or watches; they're just larger. Sitting in their own small attic room, the clockworks have the heft of nineteenth-century industrial gears. Big gears pull an oversized bicycle chain to move the weights and strike the bell, while smaller gears (or "wheels") keep the time with a gentle tick-tock. It's a combination of brute force and perfect balance, like watching a three-hundred-pound ballerina pirouetting in *Swan Lake*.

Up in the tower, the clock's ticking is reassuring. It's authoritative. It imposes order. You would never think of doubting it, as you might the measly digital numbers we see blinking at us from so many household appliances. It's almost enough to make you a believer in the "clockwork universe," the cosmos as a perfect machine.

"It keeps very, very good time," Fogg says. You can set your watch by it. And all three faces are in sync. (There's no clock on the back of the tower, which faces the cemetery. "To those people, time means nothing," he says.)

"When the clock strikes I'll look at my watch," he says. He wears a big wristwatch. "This is an atomic watch. It's right to the second. My wife told me I ought to have this because that way I keep the clock right. If I'm home and I hear it strike, I'll look at my watch and say, yep, it's right on."

It doesn't take much to stop the clock. He can lay his finger on part of the escapement—the small wheel that beats out the tick-tock—and all three clock faces, each six feet tall, stop.

As "Agent for Town Clock" (his official title—for which he's paid about $700 a year), Fogg has seen the clock through some tough times—broken strikers, stuck weights, a bent shaft, a stuck clock arm. Twice, the striker—the hammer that strikes the 1820 Revere and Son bell—has broken because someone was ringing the bell on the hour. When that happens the 1,100-pound bell smashes into the 40-pound hammer. The bell has to be sitting still on the hour when the hammer strikes, otherwise he finds a broken hammer lying on the belfry floor.

The first time that happened "I was kind of a rookie," he says, just five years on the job. When he realized that the strike hammer was broken, he figured there was no reason to keep winding the strike. He gave it a rest; the weights descended in the chute all the way to the basement. With the hammer fixed, he started to crank the heavy weights. "When I started to wind it, I said, wow, this is working hard. I thought, well, it's because the weights are all the way down and I have to wind up the weights plus the chain. So I'm cranking away and all of a sidden *bang!* I heard this loud crack. A big timber that holds one of the pulleys snapped right off." The weights were jammed. The tension built up; a big, half-inch-thick steel S-shaped hook stretched almost straight before it let go and the timber cracked; and the chain went flying. "It took me about three months to get all of that straightened out," he says.

Another time the clock was stopping at twenty-five minutes to the hour. "Just randomly. Not every hour. And I'm thinking, what the heck is making the clock stop?" He'd reset it and "the clock might work for a day. Might work for five hours. Might work for two days. All of a sudden the clock would stop twenty-five minutes to the hour."

"I spent two or three weeks coming down here, looking

at everything. Checking everything. What is doing this?" He finally found the problem: on the east clock face, there was one loose screw on the Roman numeral VII. Sometimes the minute hand would slip past that one screw, sometimes it caught it. That's all it took to stop the clock. He opened a small door in the clock face, leaned way out, and removed that screw.

But mostly it's just a matter of being faithful and attentive for nearly half a century. Fogg delicately adjusts the pendulum to compenstate for the weather, because metals expand and contract with the temperature. In the winter when the metal contracts, the clock speeds up slightly, so he adjusts the pendulum ever so slightly.

The crank handle to set the strike is worn shiny in one spot, a groove. Every time the crank comes around it rubs against the bell rope, so in 140 years the hemp has polished a little valley in the steel shaft. Bob Fogg accounts for a third of that wear. Add it up: He has been winding the clock a little more than forty-six years. That's 2,400 weeks, with 168 cranks a week . . . and Fogg has pushed that heavy crank through more than 403,000 revolutions. And add to that more than 167,000 turns to keep the time train ticking.

Constancy, routine. He's wound the clock through wars, assassinations, moon landings, riots, presidential impeachments, inflation, stagflation, recessions, the Cold War, terrorist attacks, and all the rest.

But it's not a stifling routine. It's a devotion. We count on people like this to keep all the other clocks in town running—the ones that beat out the yearly town meetings and reports and parades, the committees that attend to necessary repairs and improvements, the people who surprise us by showing us the grace of the ordinary. A quick check of Hancock's town report shows more than 125 different people volunteering for town offices and committees to keep this community of 1,650 going.

Bob Fogg comes from people who believed in community service, but they never used those words at all. It's just what you did. You pitched in and helped out. His great-great-uncle helped to raise money to buy the clock in 1872. When the town needed a water system, his grandfather helped to see to that, and when electricity arrived, he helped with that too. His grandfather ran the general store from 1896 to 1926. His grandmother taught school in town. An aunt was the first "woman selectman" in Hancock (in the Dark Ages: the 1950s).

"His grandfather just had a little bit to do with everything that was going on and everybody knew him and trusted him. Bob is like that," says a neighbor. He leads field trips to see the bell, coaches sports, is the Easter bunny, makes cookies for a fundraiser in town—it's a very long list. It's just that he's always around, doing something for the town. He doesn't say anything about it. If it needs to be done, he does it. He doesn't have a grand plan, or any ulterior motives. He won't tell you any of this, either. He doesn't smother you in ancestor talk. He keeps the clock going, just as his ancestors had helped keep the town going.

"I do it because I take pride in living in Hancock and seeing the clock work. In all the years I've been winding the clock, the only other one that's ever wound it is my son. When I started doing this, my son Bobby was about four or five years old. He used to come up with me—you know how kids follow their dad. Well, Bobby used to say to me, Dad, when you retire, when you give up this job, I'll take it over. And I said, well maybe, but I have to tell the selectmen because they have to appoint you. I just can't give you this job. So, Bobby says, you put the good word in for me."

COMING TO NEW HAMPSHIRE

When we moved to New Hampshire more than thirty years ago, we rented a little carriage house on the main street of a small town. I arrived first and unpacked our things. My wife, Sy, was living in a tent in the Australian Outback.

My first evening, I took a walk around town. There was a small historical society in an old brick schoolhouse smaller than a two-car garage, which was open only in the summer. Inside it was musty-cool, and as disheveled as an attic.

I looked at the items on the shelves. The labels were handwritten in perfect, faded, script:

"This tassel formed a part of the decorations of the funeral car which carried the remains of the late President Lincoln...."

The *late* President Lincoln. I snapped to attention. Here

was a glimpse of a community in the act of remembering. Here was a community creating its history, choosing the stories it would tell about itself, choosing its ancestors, marking out monuments and holidays—choosing who gets to enter the memory house.

Next items on the shelf: Hardtack sent home from the Civil War, a drum that may have been used in the Revolution, the parson's sermon on hearing of the death of Washington: "Know ye not that there is a prince and a great man fallen this day in Israel?" And on it went in that small space.

Memory is a defining characteristic of New England.

I came out into the twilight a little bit changed. I had studied American history in college, but I didn't move to New Hampshire to write about it. At the time I was writing for some architecture and design magazines in New York.

I kept looking around at town meetings, at Franklin Pierce and Mount Monadnock, and several years later published my first New Hampshire book, *In the Memory House*. It is a book that also takes in the lost West End of Boston, the fallen landscape of tall trees, Johnny Appleseed, Jack Kerouac, Thoreau and the Ice King, a remarkable small-town pharmacist, and the many ways we have come to live in modern times.

More summers on ponds and ridgelines, more traveling locally, and other books followed. The short essays collected here are about the same thing—learning to be a tourist of the near at hand, admitting that your homeplace is blessed, strange, surprising, and ordinary.

So although I never planned it, I'm still doing what I did my first night in New Hampshire: walking around, looking at this place, talking to people, and puzzling over and enjoying this craggy corner of New England.

Upon arriving in a new place, the mundane seems fantastic. The routine is not yet routine; it has a kind of majesty. In this way tourism is a drug. Even things like No Parking signs or crosswalks can be interesting in a new city.

In the first months after we moved to New Hampshire everything was strikingly new, as if it existed in bold outline and sharply etched colors, particularly the way Monadnock played hide and seek, appearing at the crest of a hill, at the bend of a road, across a pond. The mountain was everywhere and yet discrete.

On my second day in New Hampshire, I called the phone company to come start my phone service. I was calling from a phone booth. This was a long time ago. The man at the phone company told me that I needed to make an $11 deposit. I would have to drive to the next town and leave a check at the general store.

I wrote out the $11 check and went to the general store. The man there took my check and put it in his sparsely populated cash drawer, under the tray holding the bills. I waited a beat for a receipt or some acknowledgment. None was forthcoming. I drove back to the payphone and called the company to tell them that I'd left the deposit. "Okay," the man said, "we'll be there in two days." "Wait," I said, "How do you know that I left the deposit?" "Well, you said you did," was his answer. He could check, he said, but my word was good. (My word was worth at least $11. Modest, yes, but a good start.) And that, in short, is how things have gone in New Hampshire. It's like walking an old crooked path that proves to be the most direct route.

A few months later I was writing a magazine story about alcoholism in New Hampshire and the neighboring states—there's a lot, with five New England states among the top twenty for alcohol consumption per capita. I was looking for statistics. I forget the specifics. I called around Massachusetts looking for comparative numbers, being guided to ever-deeper recesses of the government until I reached a gravelly voiced man who probably had achieved invisibility in some sub-office basement and could have been appointed by James Michael Curley in the 1930s. Yeah, he had those statistics—that *public information*—why did I want it? Was I worthy? I would have to call back, a few times, before he gave it up.

But I couldn't find the New Hampshire statistics. Here everyone in government answered the phone and tried to be helpful. No, they didn't have the statistics. "Try so-and-so on the Seacoast," they said, naming a citizen who may have served on some committee or commission, or "try so-and-so in the Upper Valley, or . . ." and they'd dig out the phone number for me. New Hampshire was really just a big college campus. I called those folks. They were very nice. We chatted. They didn't know those statistics, but it was a good question. I should call so-and-so in the Mount Washington Valley, or so-and-so in the North Country—wait, they'd say, let me give you their number and tell them you talked to me. I probably could have called the entire state and had a nice time talking with everyone. But I didn't need to: no one had gathered the statistics. This happens in small states. Instead of relying on empirical evidence (which might revise common practice), everyone just got on with business: they followed the crooked path to the most direct solution at hand.

My neighbor told me that you should be two phone calls away from the governor. I've never called the governor, but I've called other offices and if they didn't answer, they always returned my call the next day. One time we had set up a medical savings account when that was a new thing and I needed to know what the New Hampshire rules were. I called the state insurance department. The head of the department called me back. He was really interested that we were setting up an account and he wanted to know all about it. He kept me on the phone twenty minutes, until I excused myself. He loved to talk insurance. (Oh, and this is too typical to even mention—there weren't any particular state rules. Not surprising in a state where seat belts and motorcycle helmets were not required for adults.)

Most stories about moving to "the country" usually begin like this, so forgive me. The city mouse arrives, finds the country mice to be odd, antique, and colorful, and just waiting, it turns out, for some keen-eyed city mouse to narrate their quaint folkways. But New Hampshire is not some time-out-of-mind Brigadoon that waits every four years for the national media to set up for a shot with the reporter in front of a meetinghouse or a covered bridge. (Or a fake bridge. For years the national media stayed at the Sheraton Wayfarer in Bedford, which had a small covered pedestrian bridge that looked good in the background.) New Hampshire is a place where there are layers of time, where many times coexist and swirl together. Think, if you will, of someone sitting in their 1799 farmhouse by the woodstove, answering email and streaming movies. The interstate and the dirt road, town meeting's direct democracy and our general mass malaise don't cancel each other out. The old ways aren't a lie because they are entwined with the contemporary. History, just when you think it's gone out the door, stands up and speaks eloquently and right to the point.

What is New Hampshire? It's a loose confederacy of small towns, cities, and local allegiances to lakes, ponds, and mountains. Each lake or mountain is someone's holy land. Compare this to Vermont. People love Vermont. "Vermont-ness" sells many products, from bread to teddy bears. Vermont is one of the rare states to have an identity strong enough to be a brand like Coke or Disney, says a marketing consultant. People talk about going to Vermont, but they seldom talk about New Hampshire in its totality. They talk about going to Lake Winnipesaukee or Squam Lake or the White Mountains. Watching a leaf falling in Vermont is the real thing, but watching a leaf falling in New Hampshire just means you couldn't drive far enough or find a room in Vermont. That's the skewed view of many tourists.

Vermont is more inviting for visitors. They love the valleys and views in Vermont. In New Hampshire, we're in the woods. The English geographer Jay Appleton says that we are attuned to places offering prospect and refuge. Going back to our time on Africa's savannah, we needed places to conceal ourselves and see what was coming—is that an animal I can eat? Or is it coming to eat me? We like houses that command a hill, porches with views, and long valleys with open pastures. Our primitive selves love Vermont.

New Hampshire, since the Europeans arrived, is a jostling bag of different regions. What does the Monadnock region have to say to the North Country? What does the Seacoast have to do with the Upper Valley? Are the Boston commuters in suburban Nashua really living in the same state as those in Colebrook, which is close to Canada? And if you are lucky enough to have a camp on Lake Sunapee or a house on Sugar Hill in Franconia, well, what are Concord and Keene and Durham to you?

We're all in this together—but separately, oh so separately, each of us on his or her own two or twenty or two hundred acres. The news barely travels from one town to another. I seldom get the word about surrounding towns, even though I troll the newspapers for it. Someone once described the state as being 234 "scrub brush republics." Each town is a self-contained world, each full of zeal and sloth, rumor and reform, and each as different as one family from the next. One town meeting season I went to a dozen different meetings. Each was like walking in on a family at dinner. There were old family jokes and arguments and differing outlooks and expectations. True to the old line, the happy towns were each alike in their general well being, and the unhappy towns were each unhappy in their own way.

And like all places, what's most important is invisible. I have spoken to visitors who are vexed by this invisibility. So many things that in other states are looked after by the state or the county are tended by towns and legions of volunteers. That can't be, I've been told by visitors from New York State. I understand their confusion; I grew up in Nelson Rockefeller's Empire State, a land of extensive state parks, universities, a thruway built before the interstates, and all these different semi-independent "authorities." Rocky was a kind of Republican that no longer exists. Rocky would discover that, say, there was a sneaker shortage. New Yorkers were woefully unshod. He would, with the aid of the legislature, create a state Sneaker Authority—or better yet a tri-state Sneaker Authority. It was a big era for "regional planning." The Sneaker Authority would float bonds to pay for the sneakerization of New York. These bonds were often arranged with Nelson's brother, David, who ran Chase Manhattan and got a handsome return for his bank. And then the Sneaker Authority would succeed. New Yorkers had sneakers. But it wasn't the end of the story. The Sneaker Authority now had thousands of employees and no mandate to sunset, so they looked around and broadened their mission: they would invest in shoelace factories and canvas production and rubber research and ports to bring in sneaker supplies and twin towers to encourage sneaker commerce and they'd keep floating bonds. All this worked pretty well when New York was a rich state.

New Hampshire was never a rich state—until recently. (It ranks a surprising sixth by median income, fifth by per capita income.) But poverty formed its outlook and an allergy to taxes is the state religion. Failure is the first lesson the landscape teaches. Almost everyone has ghosts for neighbors: cellar holes from failed farms, stonewalls that once edged pastures that are now left to themselves in the woods, abandoned railroad beds and bridges, ruins of mills and ruins of hard work and good intentions. Failure everywhere you look. We proceed cautiously. If there were a sneaker shortage, a bunch of neighbors would form a committee and see how they could solve the problem without raising more than a few thousand dollars.

This is how things really work in small towns. People get together, figure things out, and walk the crooked path to a solution. One woman I know told me about how she used to help an old neighbor. "He had all sorts of problems," she said. He was quite ill. "I used to pick up his urine sample every morning and take it to the hospital," she said, and added that you can't do that anymore, just waltz in with your neighbor's piss. There has to be a "chain of custody." But back then, you just did what needed to be done. This is not a heart-warming story. Norman Rockwell would never paint a picture of *The Urine Pickup*, and you won't find it in *Our Town*. But it's a New Hampshire story; it looks directly at the unpleasant facts, and takes care of them.

This may be what gives New Hampshire its case of terminal modesty. No one belts out a song saying that New Hampshire is "A-number-one, top of the list, king of the hill." No one calls it The Big Granite. Even those farmers who wrested a living from the rocky soil, and those textile manufacturers who rode the tilt-a-whirl of that industry, never boasted that if they could make it in New Hampshire, they could make it anywhere. Nope. New Hampshire takes a perverse pride in its modesty. The late Van McLeod, the state's long-serving commissioner of cultural resources, told a story about a glassblower who lived in a small town up north. The glassblower was pretty good—one of the best in the nation. Not that he impressed anyone in his town. "Him?" said a puzzled local. "He can't be that good. He's my neighbor."

FURTHER READING

꜀꜀꜀

BOOKS BY HOWARD MANSFIELD

Cosmopolis
In the Memory House
Skylark
The Same Ax, Twice
The Bones of the Earth
Turn & Jump
Dwelling in Possibility
Sheds
Where the Mountain Stands Alone (Editor)
Hogwood Steps Out (For Children)

For readers who would like to continue their visit to this corner of New Hampshire, here are a few essays about these places from Howard's other books:

ANTRIM
"Timescape: I Opened the Store as Usual" in *Turn & Jump: How Time & Place Fell Apart.*

HANCOCK

The title essay of *The Bones of the Earth*, "The Walking Stick & The Edge of the Universe," and "Boom."

"Pages from Ice Storm Journal" and "The Perilous Career of a Footpath" in *Dwelling in Possibility: Searching for the Soul of Shelter.*

"A Moment's Bright Flash" in *The Same Ax, Twice: Restoration and Renewal in a Throwaway Age.*

HARRISVILLE

"The Family History of Water" in *Turn & Jump: How Time & Place Fell Apart.*

HILLSBOROUGH

The title essay of *The Bones of the Earth* and "Big Changes in Small Places."

KEENE

"Tomorrow's Another Working Day" in *The Same Ax, Twice: Restoration and Renewal in a Throwaway Age.*

"The Bottom of the Lake" in *The Bones of the Earth.*

MOUNT MONADNOCK

"The Shrinking of the Grand Monadnoc" in *In the Memory House.*

NASHUA

"The Flaneur of the Strip" in *The Bones of the Earth.*

NEW IPSWICH

The title essay of *In the Memory House.*

"Timescape: Pasture Day" in *Turn & Jump: How Time & Place Fell Apart.*

PETERBOROUGH

"The Blueblood Milltown" and "Big Changes in Small Places" in *The Bones of the Earth.*

"The Many Mitzvahs of Myer Goldman" and "The Murder that Never Really Happened" in *In the Memory House.*

"Clarence Derby's USA" in *Turn & Jump: How Time & Place Fell Apart.*

"Building the Elephant" in *The Same Ax, Twice: Restoration and Renewal in a Throwaway Age.*

SOME NEW HAMPSHIRE INSTITUTIONS

"Old Home Day, Every Day" in *The Same Ax, Twice: Restoration and Renewal in a Throwaway Age.*

"The Museum of Democracy: Town Meeting" and "The Forgotten Sorrow of Franklin Pierce, President" in *In the Memory House.*

"The Old Homestead" in *Turn & Jump: How Time & Place Fell Apart.*

"The Otter Mates for Life" in *The Bones of the Earth.*